MANUAL

for Social Skills Training in Young People with Parent and Teacher Programmes

STOP

THINK

DO

LINDY PETERSEN
ANNE F. GANNONI

First published 1992
by The Australian Council for Educational Research Ltd
19 Prospect Hill Road, Camberwell, Melbourne, Victoria 3124
Reprinted 1993, 1994, 1996

Printed by Jenkin Buxton Printers Pty Ltd

National Library of Australia
Cataloguing-in-Publication data

Petersen, Lindy.
    Manual for social skills training in young people with parent
    and teacher programmes.

    ISBN 0 86431 116 8.

    1. Social skills — Study and teaching (Primary). 2. Social
    skills in children. I. Gannoni, Anne F. II. Australian Council
    for Educational Research. III. Title.

372.82044

Contents

Introduction

This manual is designed to provide therapists, teachers and others involved in the social development of children and adolescents with the programme content of social skills training groups for children and adolescents, and concurrent training groups for parents and teachers. Although numerous packages which aim to teach social skills to children have been produced, they have failed in the main to provide complementary parent programmes which can enhance the outcome of the children's programme. Furthermore, involvement of teachers in a complementary training programme to facilitate transfer of newly acquired skills to the school situation has been neglected.

The programme package is broad-based in that it includes the child and adolescent's critical social environments, namely home and school. It is also a multi-faceted approach which integrates several conceptual approaches to social skills training. The aim is to incorporate these features to improve the peer relations and social competence of our young people through systematic training in requisite social skills in a peer group setting, with complementary training for parents and teachers.

The child and adolescent programmes outlined in this manual are essentially an integration of Behavioural and Cognitive Social Problem Solving approaches, with emphasis also on the motivational determinants of social behaviour. The concurrent parent and teacher training programmes incorporate the same principles and methods as the children's programme.

This is a therapeutic intervention with therapists, parents, teachers and peers acting as adjunct trainers in the social skills development of target children and adolescents. Group psychodynamic processes also provide an impetus for motivational, cognitive and behavioural change in prosocial directions.

The broad-based, multi-faceted approach promotes generalization and maintenance of positive outcomes of the training programme. Additionally, the flow-over effect to other family and class members serves as a preventive intervention for these non-targeted individuals.

The first chapter provides background from the research literature regarding social skills development and training programmes for children, adolescents and parents, with a discussion of the role of teachers in training.

The second chapter contains an overview of the programmes including a discussion of aims, essential components and practical information necessary to implement the programmes.

The third chapter presents the content, a comprehensive session by session description, of a programme suitable for children aged from about 7-12 years.

Similarly, the fourth chapter contains a programme designed for young adolescents, 13-15 years of age.

The fifth chapter presents the content of the parent programme in session by session detail, while the sixth chapter traces teacher involvement and presents training details.

1

The final chapter concludes with a brief discussion on programme evaluation and possible research indications.

The appendices contain examples of assessment, evaluation and report forms used in the programme, together with information handouts regarding the programme content.

The social skills training programme package has been developed over the past 12 years by the authors in their capacity as Clinical Psychologists working with children and adolescents who experience difficulty with peer relationships due to a lack of social competence and related social skills.

The authors wish to acknowledge the valuable contribution of colleagues, particularly Mr. Phil Woodroffe in the Adelaide Children's Hospital to the development of the programmes contained in this manual.

Chapter 1:
Research Background

DEFINITION OF SOCIAL SKILLS

The diversity of theoretical frameworks, assessment procedures, treatment programmes and research indications in the field of social skills has given rise to a plethora of definitions. There are however, common elements which occur in proposed definitions (Budd, 1985). These include:—

- an emphasis on discrete learned behaviours and/or underlying cognitive skills which are considered directly related to general social competence.

- a presumption that social behaviours are evaluated as skilful relative to the specific interpersonal context in which they occur.

- a reference to the need for a balance between achieving a positive outcome for the individual (personal goal) while preserving the rights of others in the interpersonal context (prosocial goal).

For the purposes of this manual, the definition of social skills proposed by Ladd and Mize (1983) is applicable. They refer to the "ability to organize cognitions and behaviours into an integrated course of action directed toward culturally acceptable social or interpersonal goals". p.127.

This definition, supported by research, highlights the critical elements in social development, namely:—

- cognitive skills such as knowledge of appropriate social behaviour, comprehension of strategies to achieve social goals and interpersonal problem solving abilities (Asher and Renshaw, 1981; Pellegrini, 1987; Kazdin et al, 1987; Foster, 1983).

- verbal and non-verbal behavioural skills such as friendly approach behaviours and play styles, giving and accepting compliments, maintaining conversations, appropriate use of gestures, eye-contact and facial expression (Putallaz, 1983; Dodge, 1983; Christoff et al, in press; Coie and Kupersmidt, 1983; Foster, 1983; Herbert, 1986).

- prosocial motivation and goal orientation (Renshaw and Asher, 1983; Parkhurst and Asher, 1985; Krasnor and Rubin, 1981).

These social skills are indicators of social competence and effect the quality of peer relationships.

EFFECTS OF SOCIAL SKILLS DEFICITS

It has been estimated that between 5% and 15% of children in the primary school age group experience significant peer relationship problems (Hymel and Asher, 1977; French and Tyne, 1982). Also, several studies have shown a significant relationship between poor peer relations in childhood and concurrent as well as long term emotional and social maladjustment. Some children with poor social functioning also show poor academic achievement (Hartup, 1970), conduct disorders (Cox et al, 1976), hyperactivity (Pelham and Bender, 1982) social avoidance and mistreatment by peers (O'Connor, 1972) and adolescent delinquency (Freedman et al, 1978).

3

Retrospective studies have shown that children with social skills deficits and poor peer relations may have poor life adjustment as adults (Robins, 1966), with higher incidences of anti-social behaviour (Roff et al, 1972) and psychiatric disturbance (Cowen et al, 1973).

Conversely, research has indicated that children who are socially competent have demonstrated superior academic achievement (Muma, 1968) and adequate interpersonal adjustment in later life (Barclay, 1966). The implication is that quality peer relationships are essential for adequate socialization in childhood. Furthermore, when these early relationships are limited, opportunities for social interaction and thus further skills development will be restricted in adolescence and adulthood (Combs and Slaby, 1977).

Ladd and Asher (1985) and Kazdin (1985) summarize the research which, although often thwart with methodological difficulties (Parker and Asher, 1987) suggests that children with poor peer relations and poor related social skills are vulnerable to psychological, behavioural and social disorders both concurrently and in later life.

FOCUS AND FORM OF INTERVENTION

Indications of the lasting adverse effects and high incidence of poor peer relations and deficits in related social skills have served as an impetus for the development and implementation of intervention programmes to teach social skills to children and adolescents who experience or are at risk of, poor social relations, particularly isolation or rejection from their peers. The basic premises of these programmes are that peer non-acceptance is related to deficits in essential social skills, and that these skills can be trained with the result being lasting gains in positive peer relationships (Ladd, 1981; Siperstein and Gale, 1983).

The focus of intervention may vary according to the population identified. The programme may focus on therapeutic intervention for children and adolescents with identified social problems in a small group, in a clinic setting; or a preventive intervention/education for normal (primary prevention) or "at risk" children or adolescents (secondary prevention), particularly suited to a school-based setting (Pellegrini and Urbain, 1985).

Regardless of the focus of intervention, social skills training programmes typically take the form of a methodological, step by step approach to therapy and/or education. The programme is replicable and aims at generalizing and maintaining learned skills and positive outcomes outside of the training situation.

COGNITIVE - BEHAVIOURAL APPROACHES

Two major approaches incorporated in social skills training are the Behavioural and Cognitive Problem Solving approaches which are based in sound theory and research. Both generate methodological programmes suited to application in clinical and educational settings.

The Behavioural method employs techniques such as instruction, modelling, rehearsal, feedback and reinforcement (Bellack, 1979; Hops, 1983). Using these methods, children and adolescents are taught a variety of discrete social behaviours including how to initiate, maintain and terminate conversations, give and receive compliments, make positive approaches to peers, and behave assertively.

The Cognitive Problem Solving method (pioneered by Spivack and Shure, 1974) focusses on training covert cognitive processes rather than discrete behavioural patterns. Specifically, children are taught to identify interpersonal problems, generate alternative strategies for these problems, evaluate these solutions by considering their consequences and finally, plan and execute the action of choice. As part of this process, the child's knowledge and comprehension of appropriate or normative strategies for use in interpersonal interactions is enhanced.

Difficulties have been encountered with both approaches outlined. Cognitive problem solving programmes which do not include direct training in behavioural skills or behavioural reinforcement contingencies in and outside of the training setting do not consistently produce positive outcomes in terms of social adjustment in the natural environment (Kendall and Braswell, 1985; Rickel et al, 1983). On the other hand, Behavioural approaches often fail to generalize positive gains across different contexts, and maintain gains over time (Kazdin, 1985; Stark, 1987). Since the Cognitive Problem Solving approach utilizes more pervasive and underlying cognitive skills, generalization outside of the original teaching environment is more likely and has been substantiated by research (Spivack and Shure, 1974; Elias et al, 1986). Moreover, research has also shown the viability of the Cognitive approach as a primary preventive, competence-building method for use with larger groups in the school classroom (Weissberg et al, 1981; Gesten et al, 1982). This approach enables social skills to be taught within the school curriculum to normal children who are functioning reasonably well. The acquisition of these additional skills will help them cope with a variety of social problems in everyday life (Meichenbaum et al, 1983).

Several studies have demonstrated the particular effectiveness of combining elements of the Cognitive Problem Solving and Behavioural approaches. (McGillivray 1983; Kendall and Braswell, 1982; Lochman et al, 1984; Kazdin et al, 1987). In this combined method, behavioural techniques are used to suppress deviant behaviours and to model, roleplay and rehearse effective strategies. Behavioural reinforcement contingencies are also built in to the programme. Concurrently, children are taught how to think about, evaluate and choose solutions to interpersonal problems before they initiate behaviour.

MOTIVATIONAL DETERMINANTS OF SOCIAL BEHAVIOUR

Recent research has highlighted the underlying motivational processes which elicit social behaviour and thereby effect peer relations by influencing the choice of strategies and actions made in each social situation encountered (Renshaw and Asher, 1983; Taylor and Asher, 1984). A fundamental task confronting a child or adolescent in a social situation is to decide on which goal(s) from a number of relevant personal and interpersonal goals to pursue.

The implication for social skills training programmes is that focus be placed not only on the acquisition, practice and generalization of new cognitive and behavioural skills, but also on changes in the goal orientation of the child or adolescent (Parkhurst and Asher, 1985).

Related to the motivational determinants of social behaviour is the confidence children have in their own social skills and in their ability to achieve their goals by using these skills in social interactions (Wheeler and Ladd, 1982). Practicing social skills and achieving social goals generally evokes positive social feedback. This builds self-confidence, and plays an important role in the outcome of social skills training programmes.

In summary, research indications are for a multi-faceted approach to social skills training for children and adolescents, including:—

- *verbal and non-verbal behavioural skills training*
- *cognitive problem solving skills training based on sound knowledge and comprehension of socially appropriate strategies*
- *motivational change through goal modification in a socially acceptable (prosocial) direction.*

5

GENERALIZATION AND MAINTENANCE: A BROAD-BASED APPROACH

The issue of transfer of newly acquired skills to environments and interpersonal contexts outside of the original learning situation has been a major one for researchers and practitioners in this field. Research suggests that guided practice of newly acquired social skills in the child's natural environment may be critical for transfer of skills (Pellegrini and Urbain, 1985). For this to occur, environmental supports must be available to the child or adolescent which can reinforce rather than extinguish newly learned skills (Bagarozzi, 1985).

For most children and young adolescents, these environmental supports are most likely to be located in the family and school systems. Thus, social skills training programmes provided for children and adolescents without the involvement of significant others in these support systems may considerably limit the maintenance and generalization of positive outcomes achieved in the children's programme (Kendall and Braswell, 1982; McGillivray, 1983; Budd, 1985). These programmes will therefore optimally broaden their base to include family members, school staff and students.

Parents particularly represent a valuable source of manpower in a training programme as they are able to provide constant, relevant, long term instruction to their child. Because parents are capable of teaching various patterns of behaviour to their children, they are presumably capable of teaching social skills which may be maintained over time and reinforced over many different social settings in which parents interact with their children.

Furthermore, by educating parents about social behaviour and requisite social skills and involving them actively in training and skills transfer, the quality of relationships within the family which influences the child's social functioning in other areas of life,will be enhanced.

PARENTS AS MEDIATORS IN SOCIAL SKILLS TRAINING

Parent management programmes have typically emphasized behavioural techniques with social learning principles as a base. Parents are taught to positively reinforce social behaviours, use modelling, shaping and instruction to train new skills, ignore many misbehaviours and exert consistent logical or natural consequences for behaviour (Patterson, 1982). Because social skills training utilizes social communication skills especially reflective listening, cognitive problem solving strategies, and social goal setting and evaluation, it is also relevant to include these elements in the parent training programme. A widely used example of this approach is the Systematic Training for Effective Parenting programme, designed by Dinkmeyer and McKay (1976).

When used on their own, parent training programmes containing these elements are, to a certain extent effective in promoting lasting gains in social development for the children of the parents involved (Kazdin, 1985). However, Kazdin et al, (1987) reported on the improved benefits of combining an **effective** parent management training programme simultaneously with an **effective** cognitive-behavioural social skills training programme for children. The benefits were shown in positive gains in prosocial behaviour and adjustment, generalized gains to school and home environments, and maintained gains over one (1) year following training.

Budd (1985) recognized the merits of using parents as "adjunct trainers", participating in a training programme concurrent with a social skills training programme for children. The role of the parent is in training, reinforcing and maintaining target social skills in the home and related environments. Parents demonstrate learned skills adapted to the family situation, set up regular practice situations at home, and actively reinforce skilled behaviour in a variety of settings. Since parents receive regular instruction and systematic monitoring as adjunct trainers in a clinic or school based training programme, the extent of their involvement and responsibility as trainers can be varied to obtain the maximum benefit for the child or adolescent.

Shure and Spivack (1978) found that a child's problem solving skills and strategies even when used outside of their home are related to those of their parents. Thus, training the parents in effective social problem solving skills has beneficial effects for the child by promoting effective skills development, and by changing the child's social environment in the way the parents react and relate to the child which may be contributing to poor social behaviour.

The training package contained in this manual combines a Parent Management Training programme and a Cognitive-Behavioural Social Skills Training programme for children and adolescents. Moreover, the parent programme incorporates the critical elements of the children's programme. These include the cognitive social problem solving method and the achievement of prosocial goals for both children and parents.

In summary, the parent training programme serves a multi-purpose:—

- *a cognitive-behavioural social skills training programme for the parents themselves.*
- *a parent-mediated therapeutic intervention with parents as adjunct trainers in teaching social skills to their children.*
- *a broader base for generalization and maintenance of positive outcome of the children's programme.*
- *a preventive intervention for siblings of the target child or adolescent.*

TEACHERS AS MEDIATORS IN SOCIAL SKILLS TRAINING

Teachers are in a viable position to assist in the social skills development of their students on a regular basis and generally in a more objective manner than is possible for parents. Teachers have expertise and training in implementing educational programmes with groups of children and adolescents, and are aware of the basic principles of learning and behaviour modification included in social skills training. Moreover, they are uniquely privy to the peer interactions of children and adolescents outside of the family influence. They see children in a wider variety of peer-related contexts in which they are readily able to set up training and practice situations.

Research supports this view that the school is an ideal setting for therapeutic and preventive efforts to train the social skills of young people (Allen et al, 1976; Elias et al, 1986).

In the package contained in this manual, the critical elements of the cognitive-behavioural programme for children and adolescents are incorporated in a concurrent teacher training programme.

In summary, the teacher training programme serves a multi-purpose:—

- *education in social skills for teachers themselves.*
- *a teacher-mediated, therapeutic intervention with teachers as adjunct trainers in the social skills development of the target child or adolescent in their class.*
- *a broader base for generalization and maintenance of positive outcomes of the children's programme.*
- *a preventive intervention for non-targeted class members.*

PEERS AS MEDIATORS IN SOCIAL SKILLS TRAINING

The research into the adverse effects of poor peer relationships on personal and social adjustment underlines the central role peers play in the socialization process. Social skills training programmes however, have generally failed to utilize this powerful influence.

Some research (Strain and Fox, 1981; Hops, 1983) has shown the efficacy of involving peers as trainers in social skills acquisition, generalization and maintenance, particularly through modelling and shared reinforcement contingencies with the target child. The context of training the target child and the peers who will continue in the role as trainers should resemble the environment to which generalization is geared, for example the classroom, schoolyard or community group setting.

Furthermore, by involving the child's peers in the actual training process, their generally resistant preconceptions, expectations and reactions to the target child may be modified to allow for recognition and support of the child's newly acquired social skills. The research is loaded with examples of social skills training programmes with positive outcomes which do not transfer to the natural peer related environment due to a history of negative peer interactions with the target child and/or the presence of similarly deficient socially unresponsive peers (Strain and Fox, 1981; Lochman et al, 1984). Without specific programming involving peers as targets for training and as potential trainers, generalization and maintenance of social skills in the natural peer related environment may not be expected to occur.

In summary, the social skills training package outlined in this manual utilizes age peers as follows:—

- *Group peers — as adjunct trainers in a peer mediated therapeutic intervention through the shared development of social skills in a group learning/socializing context which closely resembles school and community based peer related environments.*

- *School peers — as supports in the classroom receiving training input via their teacher's instruction and mediating role in the social skills training of the target child or adolescent in the class.*

- *Group and School peers — as a broader base for generalization and maintenance of outcomes from the children's programme.*

PSYCHODYNAMIC FACTORS IN GROUP TRAINING

The focus of the training programmes in this manual is on **group** learning and therapy. The psychodynamic processes operative in functional groups are relevant to outcomes from these programmes, a factor which is understated in the social skills training literature.

The role of the group leaders/therapists is an active one, engaging and goal oriented, as well as knowledgeable in the programme. As in most psychotherapeutic encounters, the leaders need to be warm, supportive, non-judgemental and patient to promote confidence in children, adolescents and their parents, ensuring that they maintain their involvement in the programmes (Ladd and Mize, 1983; Schrodt, 1987). Such factors influence the way children, adolescents and parents view, interpret and evaluate the therapeutic experience, which may effect the outcome of the training programmes (Kendall, 1985).

Psychodynamic processes involved in the development of group cohesion, identity, role status, group problem solving and decision making operate to create an atmosphere which will facilitate social skills development in individual members to varying degrees. The relationship between peer group members is crucial as they provide feedback and vicarious reinforcement which supports skill acquisition and goal achievement.

- *The training programmes contained in the manual aim at utilizing group psychodynamic processes to promote behavioural, cognitive and motivational change in the individuals involved.*

SOCIAL SKILLS TRAINING FOR YOUNG ADOLESCENTS

Although a great deal of research has been conducted into social skills training for preadolescent children, there has been a paucity of research into effective training methods with adolescents (Kelly, 1987).

Early adolescence brings changes in patterns of social interaction. Peer relations are extended and are generally more intense with the development of strong needs to belong to the peer group. Family relations alter as the primary frame of reference for the young adolescent shifts outside of the family. New social situations are encountered which place new demands on the young adolescent and require new skills or the refinement of existing ones. These situations include encounters with the opposite sex, part-time job experiences, taking responsibility without adult supervision, facing moral dilemmas.

Young adolescents with poor peer relationships, like younger children, have been found to have social skills deficits of a cognitive and behavioural nature, for example in their social problem solving skills, conversational skills, approach behaviours, control of aggression and disruptiveness (Christoff et al, in press; Freedman et al, 1987; Horowitz, 1982; Schrodt, 1987; Furnham, 1986). Another correlate of poor social functioning in young adolescents is the frequency and quality of personal participation in, and exposure to social activities with peers. Thus, social skills training for adolescents may need to include non-threatening, non-judgemental practice situations in peer-related social contexts (Kelly, 1987).

In summary, the training programme contained in this manual provides young adolescents with:—

- *social skills training using a cognitive-behavioural problem solving approach.*
- *a focus on the development of prosocial motivation and goal achievement within a supportive therapeutic peer group.*
- *practice in natural social environments.*
- *a broader base for skills transfer and maintenance through the involvement of parents and teachers as adjunct trainers in the therapeutic intervention.*

ASSESSMENT AND EVALUATION IN SOCIAL SKILLS TRAINING

Since the training programme outlined in this manual represents a multi-faceted and broad-based approach, the measures used to assess social skills and to evaluate the efficacy of the programme in training social skills, reflect this diversity.

The level of assessment and evaluation adopted is the General Impact Level described by Kendall et al, 1981. Social competence and peer acceptance as well as the degree of change following social skills training intervention are measured by their impact on significant others in the child or adolescent's environment. Multi-measures of general impact may usefully be obtained from parents, teachers, peers and the child/adolescent self.

Since research has indicated that parent, teacher, peer and self reports are independent, a wide sampling of opinions using different methods of assessment is suggested (Kazdin, 1985).

In the programmes contained in this manual, general impact measures obtained from rating scales and sociometric methods are used to assess:—

- the social skills of the target child/adolescent.
  (What is the child like?)
- the degree of peer acceptance.
  (Is the child liked?) (Parker and Asher, 1987).
- the impact of intervention.
- the generalization of intervention impact to home and school.
- the maintenance of impact at follow up.

THE PROGRAMMES IN PERSPECTIVE

The social skills training programme contained in this manual incorporates the following elements in a multi-faceted, broad-based approach:—

- for children and adolescents, a cognitive-behavioural problem solving programme.
- for parents, a concurrent training programme including critical elements of the child/adolescent programme to enhance skills transfer and maintenance in the home related environment and provide a preventive flow-over to siblings in the home.
- for teachers, a complementary training programme including critical elements of the child/adolescent programme to enhance transfer to the school environment and provide a preventive flow-over effect to school peers in the class.
- emphasis on motivational antecedents of social behaviour through prosocial goal orientation.
- utilization of group psychodynamics and peer mediation to bring about behavioural, cognitive and motivational change in a prosocial direction.

Chapter 2
Overview

Chapter 2:
Overview

GENERAL AIMS

Child/Adolescent Programme

- to alleviate distress for children and adolescents with difficulties in interpersonal relations and social interactions.
- to foster social competence and peer acceptance through the development of specific behavioural and cognitive social or interpersonal skills.
- to foster social competence and peer acceptance through the development of prosocial goal orientation and motivation.
- to prevent possible current and long-term aversive consequences of social skills deficits.

Parent Programme

- to provide parents with support and training in the necessary skills to act confidently and competently as adjunct trainers in the social skills development of their children.
- to enhance the development of the parents' own social, interpersonal skills for their children to imitate.
- to promote the generalization and maintenance of skills learned by the children in home related environments.
- to enhance the quality of family relationships and prevent the development of social skill deficits in siblings of the target children.

Teacher Programme

- to enlist the support of teachers to act as reinforcers for the skills learned by the children and adolescents in the group.
- to provide support and training in the necessary skills to act as adjunct trainers in the social skills development of the target children and adolescents.
- to enhance the generalization and maintenance of these skills in school related environments.
- to educate teachers in a practical and replicable approach to social skills training which, when applied in the general classroom, may prevent social skills deficits in a large proportion of children or adolescents they teach.

SPECIFIC AIMS

Child/Adolescent Programme

- to teach children and adolescents to recognize, label and accept feelings in themselves and others, and to understand the causal relationship between feelings and interpersonal events and behaviour.

- to increase their social perception skills, including actively listening to and looking at others so that they may be aware of individual differences and goals, and thereby appreciate the perspective of others.

- to develop the verbal and non-verbal behaviours necessary for effective interpersonal interactions, including conversation, communication and self-assertion skills.

- to teach interpersonal cognitive problem solving skills, including the ability to identify and define social problems and personal or social goals, generate their own solutions, consider consequences of alternatives, make decisions, implement and evaluate solutions.

- to promote awareness and comprehension of socially appropriate, normative strategies for social conflict resolution.

- to foster group membership skills, including active participation, co-operation, leadership and group decision making skills.

- to provide a supportive and reasonably structured environment for children and adolescents to practice newly learned social skills, with encouragement to apply them to their broader social environments.

- to determine for each child and adolescent the motivational basis, the nature and direction of their goals in social interactions, and to modify these in a prosocial direction through continual personal feedback within the group environment.

- to develop self esteem and self-confidence through the identification and achievement of specific personal and interpersonal goals.

- to consider moral issues involving questions of responsibility to other people and society in general.

- to encourage children and adolescents to take the initiative in forming and maintaining friendships with peers.

Parent Programme

- to determine and commit to achieving, specific goals parents have for themselves and their children.

- to instruct parents in concepts of social learning and behaviour development, including the purposes of misbehaviour and problem ownership.

- to enhance communication between parents and children through teaching skills such as open, reflective listening and I-messages.

- to instruct parents in the interpersonal cognitive problem solving skills approach and promote the utilization of these skills with, and by their children.

- to foster the use of positive management strategies such as encouragement, and natural and logical consequences.

- to provide a supportive group environment for parents to practice strategies and skills presented.

- to provide a group problem solving atmosphere to identify and discuss appropriate management strategies for specific problems they are experiencing at home.
- to monitor the application by parents of appropriate management strategies, thus determining skill acquisition and generalization by parents in their home environment.
- to provide continual feedback to parents regarding their children's progress in the group, with parents providing feedback to the children's group leaders about progress at home and in the local community.

Teacher Programme

- to instruct teachers in the interpersonal cognitive problem solving approach to social skills training, and its adaptability for use in solving social conflict in the school setting.
- to determine the particular goals the teachers have for children and adolescents in the programme, and compare these to goals set by parents and the children themselves.
- to provide regular feedback to teachers, and obtain feedback from teachers about the children's progress towards the attainment of identified social goals.
- to encourage teachers to regularly reinforce and model social skills in peer and teacher-child interactions within the classroom and school related environments.

ADMINISTRATIVE PROCESS

Referrals

Children considered appropriate for referral to a social skills group are those demonstrating difficulties with interpersonal relationships. Problems range from the socially withdrawn, shy or isolated child to the verbally or physically aggressive child. Frequently, the child is unable to cope with teasing from peers or alternatively, initiates teasing of others. Some children referred act immaturely and others are attention-seeking or demanding. Generally, they have difficulty making or maintaining friendships and are not well accepted by their peers.

A referral form is completed by the referring person (Appendix I, Referral Form) and sent to the co-ordinator of the programme who assesses the appropriateness of the referral. If suitable, the child's name is placed on a waiting list according to age (Appendix 2, Waiting List). If not an appropriate referral, the referring person is notified.

Selection Process

Children are accepted into the group if they have mild, moderate or severe difficulties with peer relations, yet not extreme behaviour problems which would overly disrupt the group.

As there is a strong conceptual component in the programme which increases in complexity with age, and as age appropriate interactions are encouraged as well, referred children are initially grouped into three age categories:—

7 - 9 years
10 - 12 years
13 - 15 years.

At the beginning of each term, the programme co-ordinator convenes a meeting between interested group leaders to check the waiting lists and select the age group for the term's programme. The age limits are flexible with some younger or older children being accepted, depending on their ability to cope cognitively or behaviourally.

To maximize the potential for children to learn positive skills from each other through peer modelling, care is taken to balance the number of children displaying aggressive and withdrawn behaviours. A group composed only of socially withdrawn children may require continual input from leaders to model skills with limited peer interactions occurring. On the other hand, a group of aggressively behaved children may demand constant behaviour management from leaders, leaving little time for social skills training.

Persons who referred the children are notified when a place is to be offered to the child and parents. Referees are encouraged to maintain contact with the family and the leaders of the social skills and parent groups during the programme, if appropriate.

Pre Group Planning

Two leaders are required for the child/adolescent groups to manage difficult behaviour, deal with problem situations as they arise, allow for small group and individual problem solving, demonstrate skills and reinforce individual goals. Two leaders are preferable in the parent group to provide alternative views and feedback, and demonstrate techniques essential to the programme, for example modelling, active listening or effective communication.

Group leaders plan session times and organize rooms. One room is required for parents, and for children in the 7 - 12 year groups, a large room which includes a versatile play area and is ideally soundproofed. Alternatively, free play may occur in an outdoor area. A one-way screen is also recommended to allow for observation by parents, trainees or teachers. Adolescent groups require a room with comfortable seating.

Letters are sent to the parents of 8 children/adolescents on the waiting list, offering group placement for child and parent (Appendix 3 Invitation to Attend). Families are asked to confirm their attendance by a specified date. If there is no response or a child is unable to attend, a place may be offered to another child on the list. Children and/or parents who have queries or seem reluctant to attend may be provided with an information booklet (Appendix 4 Information Booklet for Children and Parents).

A group size of six (6) children and two (2) leaders is optimal for the 7 — 12 year olds. Adolescent groups can accommodate eight (8) children.

The Term of the Group

Optimally, the groups run over a ten week period and are held once a week for two (2) hours.

PARENT INVOLVEMENT

In the first session, parents are asked to complete forms assessing the children's social difficulties and identifying goals for group attendance for their children and themselves (Appendix 5 Parent Form: PRE GROUP). Consent is also sought allowing group leaders to involve teachers in the programme and to videotape the children in the group.

From midway through the term, parents (preferably two (2) per week) are invited to join the children's group to participate in the social problem solving exercises presented to the children. The primary goal of such parent involvement is to aid transfer of skills gained in the group to the home situation. This level of involvement is not appropriate for adolescent groups.

During the term, spouses, caregivers and others interested in the children or adolescents, who are unable to attend weekly sessions are offered two sessions **after hours** together with the regular attenders. This offers an opportunity to further discuss and evaluate the training programmes and to enlist the support and involvement of significant others in the children's natural environment.

In session 9, parents complete post group evaluation forms (Appendix 6 Parent Form: POST GROUP).

For session 10, children do not attend but parents meet with leaders from both groups to evaluate the attainment of goals by children and parents within the group setting, at home and (for the child or adolescent) at school. Suggestions are offered for follow-up and a review date is set for three (3) months hence.

It is suggested that parents who miss sessions be contacted by group leaders to enquire about reasons for their absence and encourage their attendance. Consideration may be given to charging a fee, part of which may be refunded if attendance is maintained.

TEACHER INVOLVEMENT

After the first session, leaders of the child/adolescent group visit the schools to discuss with teachers the children's social difficulties and the aims of the social skills training programme. If there are two leaders, each may take responsibility for teacher contact for half the group members. Teachers receive printed information on the training programme (Appendix 8 General Information Leaflet), together with forms assessing the children's social difficulties and identifying goals for group attendance from the teachers' perspective (Appendix 9 Teacher Form: PRE GROUP).

At the teacher training sessions in weeks 3 and 6, the basic principles and methods of the programme are presented in depth. The goal is to enlist the teachers' co-operation in applying these principles in the classroom, while specifically supporting and reinforcing the target children to do the same. In these sessions, each teacher is also given the opportunity to focus on the individual child's difficulties and is encouraged to formulate goals accordingly. Teachers are invited to contact leaders during the term of the group for further discussion.

Following session 9, school visits are arranged by leaders to obtain feedback on the children's progress towards goal attainment in the school setting. Teachers complete post group evaluation forms (Appendix 10 Teacher Form: POST GROUP). Teachers are encouraged to maintain contact with group leaders if further concerns arise prior to the review session in three (3) months time.

CHILD/ADOLESCENT INVOLVEMENT

At the beginning of the first session, children/adolescents are asked to complete forms assessing their social difficulties and identifying their goals for group attendance (Appendix 12 Self Report Form: PRE GROUP).

Children/adolescents attend for 9 sessions of the social skills training programme.

In mid-term, adolescents are involved in a practice situation in the natural environment outside the usual group setting.

The leaders from the child/adolescent and parent groups meet following sessions 2, 5, 7, 9 to formulate and revise goals for individual children in the light of information continually received from parents, teachers, group peers and the children themselves.

At the final session for children/adolescents (Week 9), they complete post group evaluation forms which monitor progress and goal attainment (Appendix 13 Self Report Form: POST GROUP).

Following Week 10, the leaders of the child/adolescent group complete written summaries of the teacher/parent/child/group leaders' reports on goal achievement, and follow up recommendations (Appendix 15 Social Skills Programme Evaluation Report). These summary reports are made available to parents, teachers and referring persons.

SCHOOL PEER INVOLVEMENT (for 7 - 12 year olds).

If permission is forthcoming from the parent, teacher and school principal, the level of peer acceptance of each child in the group is assessed and monitored on a rating scale presented to the child's classmates (Appendix 16 Peer Rating Form: PRE/POST/REVIEW).

The peer ratings of the child's likability and acceptability as a playmate or friend reflect the child's social competence or skilfulness in various social interactions with age mates. Improved skilfulness gained in the training programme will hopefully lead to improved peer acceptance which will be reflected in the sociometric ratings obtained from school peers.

The rating form is completed by peers after sessions 1 and 9, and prior to the three (3) month review, providing a monitoring period of almost six (6) months. The peer group involvement in assessment as outlined, is not designed for adolescent groups.

School peers receive varying degrees of indirect input from the social skills training programme via teachers' instruction and modelling, and from information feedback by the target children. Teachers are encouraged to enlist the co-operation and support of school peers to reinforce, model and provide feedback regarding newly acquired social skills.

Review

Three months after the completion of the group programme, concurrent group sessions are held for parents and children/adolescents to review progress and goal maintenance in home and school environments. Parents are sent reminder letters (Appendix 17: Review Letter) about three (3) weeks prior to the meeting.

Prior to the session, school visits are arranged where ratings of peer acceptance (for 7 — 12 year olds) are obtained and review evaluation forms completed by teachers (Appendix 11 Teacher Form: REVIEW).

At the review meeting, parents and children/adolescents complete review forms (Appendix 7 Parent Form: REVIEW; Appendix 14 Self Report Form: REVIEW). Further recommendations are made and brief reports given to referring persons.

Administrative Process Flow-Chart

PRE GROUP PLANNING

Referring Person

Referral Form received ——— If not appropriate ————————————————→

    if appropriate

Child placed on waiting list

Co-ordination meeting to plan group

Invitations to attend sent

Response from family ———————————— No ————————————→

    Yes

THE TERM OF THE GROUP

Week 1:   Parent and Self Report Forms: PRE GROUP.

                School visit — Teacher Forms: PRE GROUP.
                                — Peer Rating Forms (PRE) 7 — 12 year olds.

Week 2:   Leaders' meeting.
                Spouse/caregiver session.

Week 3:   Teacher training session.

Week 5, 6,
    7 & 8:   Parents join 7 — 12 year old group.

Week 5:   Real life practice for adolescents.
                Leaders' meeting.

Week 6:   Teacher training session.

Week 7:   Leaders' meeting.
                Spouse/caregiver session.

Week 9:   Final session for children/adolescents.
                Parent and Self Report Forms: POST GROUP.
                School visit — Teacher Forms: POST GROUP.
                                — Peer Rating Forms (POST) 7 - 12 year olds.
                Leaders' meeting.

Week 10:   Final session for parents.
                Recommendations for follow up.
                Review date set.
                Social Skills Programme Evaluation Report. ———————→

REVIEW: at three (3) months.

Review letter (three (3) weeks prior).
School visit (one (1) week prior) — Teacher Forms: REVIEW
                                    — Peer Rating Forms (REVIEW) 7 — 12 year olds.

Concurrent sessions for parents and children/adolescents.
Parent and Self Report Forms: REVIEW
Further recommendations.
Final Report. ————————————————————————→

FORMAT FOR GROUPS

Child Groups (7 — 12 years)

Each group session has two major sections. The first section (about 1½ hours) includes direct instruction using discussion, roleplays, videos, and problem solving exercises. The second section, free play time (20 minutes) offers children the opportunity to practice and apply the principles learned in the first section. Leaders observe and reinforce the children for appropriate behaviour, and for using the STOP-THINK-DO approach in the play situation.

In the final five minutes of each session, homework exercises to remind the children of concepts introduced in the weekly session are presented. These exercises are placed in books to be returned each week.

A programme suitable for groups of children aged 7 — 9 years and 10 — 12 years is presented in Chapter 3 with alternative activities for younger and older children.

Adolescent Groups (13 — 15 years).

The format presented for adolescent group sessions is more flexible with no clearly defined formal learning and informal play sections. With adolescents, formal instruction and skills training is interspersed with informal conversation about their personal experience and their adaptation of principles learned in the weekly sessions.

Formal homework exercises are set. Young people are also encouraged to keep a diary of real-life problem situations, their feelings, goals and coping strategies, which they may offer for discussion in the group sessions. Exercise books are provided to be brought back each week.

Chapter 4 presents a programme suitable for young adolescents, incorporating the essentials of the cognitive problem solving approach to social skills training within a more flexible format.

Parent Groups.

The format for the parent group sessions is flexible, containing a training section and a personal feedback section. New concepts and techniques are presented each week, with formal homework assignments set, focussing on these principles. At the commencement of each session, parents report on their utilization of techniques in the home environment. Each parent is given an opportunity to observe the formal learning section of the children's group. As revision occurs, parents do not miss concepts covered during their absence from the group.

In the personal feedback section, parents have the opportunity to present current problem situations for discussion and problem solving. Principles and techniques are presented by group leaders in a supportive, non-judgemental manner so that participants feel comfortable to try techniques. It is necessary for the leader to focus on parents' positive attempts, and provide constructive feedback. Questions and comments from group members to the leader are redirected to parents to promote discussion and provide feedback to each other.

Chapter 5 contains a programme for parents which is complementary with the children's programmes in Chapters 3 and 4.

Teacher Groups.

The group sessions for teachers have two major sections.

The training section includes direct instruction in the interpersonal cognitive problem solving method using examples, practice exercises, roleplays and videos. Teachers play an active role in generating examples of social problem situations from their experiences with the children/ adolescents in the group.

The feedback section involves a discussion of goals for individual children and plans for achieving these goals in the school setting.

Chapter 6 contains a programme for teacher involvement and training which complements the programmes for children, adolescents and their parents.

PROBLEM SOLVING COMPONENT

The formal introduction of the problem solving method occurs in Session 4 of the child group, session 3 of the adolescent and parent groups, and session 1 for teachers.

A traffic light motto and the phrase STOP-THINK-DO is incorporated in this presentation. This motto may be displayed in poster form for repeated reference during the group term (Appendix 18).

The STOP-THINK-DO problem solving method is as follows:—

Reminds the children to stop before they rush into anything, consider the problem and how they and others are feeling, and what they want to happen in the situation.

Reminds the children to think about and generate many possible alternative solutions to the problem.

Solutions may involve
- fighting/forcing
- telling an adult
- demanding
- asking nicely
- bargaining
- sharing/compromising
- walking away

Think of the consequences of each solution and how the people involved may feel about the consequences.

Reminds the children to finally choose the best solution (i.e. the one with the most acceptable consequences) and put it into action to solve social problems.

If the solution does not work, go back to STOP and work through as above.

Children/adolescents are encouraged to apply this principle to all social problems (e.g. being the victim of teasing, having no-one to play with, not being allowed to do what they want by parents or teachers, responding to peer pressure).

Parents and teachers are taught this problem solving method as a multi-purpose tool for

— Handling their own behaviour management and inter-personal problems with the child/adolescent.

— Modelling appropriate social problem solving skills for the child/adolescent.

— Guiding the child through the problem solving sequence, reinforcing their newly acquired skills in the home or school environments.

STRATEGY EVALUATION COMPONENT

Once the STOP-THINK-DO process has been presented as a step by step problem solving sequence, the children/adolescents are then encouraged to focus on the THINK stage, specifically on the generation and evaluation of different solutions or strategies to the social conflict. A number of criteria are presented to assist in evaluating the solutions suggested.

A major criterion is the distinction between COOL, WEAK and AGGRO ways of behaving in social situations (Appendix 19).

THE WEAK WAY is to:—

> Talk softly, mumble.
> Cry or sulk when faced with a problem.
> Look down at the floor.
> Stand far away, hunched over.
> Give into others.
> Feel shy, embarrassed, nervous, useless, unhappy.

THE AGGRO WAY is to:—

> Shout, yell.
> Speak rudely, abuse, tease, put down.
> Look mad.
> Stand close and threaten.
> Push, hit, kick.
> Feel angry, annoyed, out of control.

THE COOL WAY is to:—

> Speak firmly but friendly.
> Stand up for yourself politely.
> Smile or look calm.
> Stand tall.
> Look other person in the eyes.
> Feel happy, confident, in control, okay about yourself.

These concepts are introduced in Session 5 of the child and parent groups, Session 4 of the adolescent group and Session 2 of the teacher group. During subsequent sessions, strategies for problem solving are categorized according to COOL/WEAK/AGGRO ways of behaving. In addition, the consequences of each proposed action are evaluated in terms of their acceptability to the people involved. The COOL way generally has the most acceptable consequences, and is therefore often the solution to choose and act on first.

A second criterion presented to the children and adolescents (Session 6) for describing and evaluating strategies is termed the FRIENDLY way. This way involves a consideration of and fairness to others which requires them to take the perspective or role of the other people in the situation. A further criterion refers to behaving in the RIGHT way, meaning the responsible course of action according to the expectations and mores of society. This criterion is introduced in Session 7 of the child and adolescent groups.

When a group problem needs resolution, children are encouraged to evaluate strategies according to a criterion termed the CO-OPERATIVE way which balances individual needs with those of others to achieve the purposes and function of the group. This criterion is discussed specifically in Session 8 of the child and adolescent groups.

Each of the descriptive/evaluative criteria make implications regarding the consequences of behaving in that way. Which consequences are most acceptable and therefore which strategies will be acted upon, depends considerably on the goal value and orientation of the individuals considering the strategies and consequences. The criteria are an abbreviated means of conceptualizing strategies and making quick implications about likely consequences. They assist in 'short-cutting' the process once the STOP-THINK-DO sequence is well practiced.

MOTIVATIONAL COMPONENT

It is apparent that the efficacy of social skills training programmes depends on the motivation of the child, adolescent and parent to pursue prosocial goals and to attain social competency. Therefore, definition of the goals individuals have for attendance at the group programme is as important as the identification of discrete social behaviours or skills required for the development of social competency. Furthermore identification of the goals, aims and concerns individuals have in **specific** interpersonal situations requires consideration to provide a more comprehensive assessment of the motivational base of participants in the programmes.

An attempt is made in session 1 of the groups to identify the goal direction of children and parents via the identified reasons for attending the social skills programme and the outcomes they hope to achieve. Note is also taken of the teachers' goal orientation by identifying the goals they wish the children or adolescents to achieve by group attendance. Moreover, a commitment is sought from all concerned to the attainment of these identified goals directed towards improved social acceptance and competency.

The group programme outlined in this manual allows for individual planning towards goal achievement for each child, adolescent and parent involved. For any individual however, social motivation, i.e. goal value and direction varies constantly. Thus, discrete personal and interpersonal goals and behaviours are regularly identified, monitored, and modified in the group sessions through direct reinforcement and personal feedback in the supportive group environment. This process is specifically described in sessions 3 and 6, for the child group; in diary entries and sessions 2, 3, 5 and 8, for the adolescent group; in sessions 2, 6, and 8 of the parent group; and both teacher training sessions.

The achievement of important personal and interpersonal goals also promotes self confidence and self esteem which serve to further motivate the pursuance of goals.

To further identify each child/adolescent's goal orientation in social interactions, they are asked to indicate **what they want to happen** in the specific social problem situations which are presented in the course of the group programme. Generally, social conflicts arise when the people involved have different or incompatible goals. This divergence is reflected in the way each person defines the problem and how he/she feels about it. By analyzing the alternative solutions for achieving the identified goals of individuals concerned and the possible consequences which might result from these actions, they receive feedback about the viability of their goals in **that** social situation.

Sound knowledge and comprehension of normative or appropriate social strategies and goals are developed through this process. Following involvement in situations which have aversive consequences resulting from the pursuit of socially maladaptive goals, the individual is encouraged to refine goals and behaviours which will lead to more acceptable consequences for the individual and hopefully society in general. The development of this evaluative process is a focus of the social skills training programme.

21

ASSESSMENT — EVALUATION COMPONENT

The forms utilized in the programme package serve two (2) functions. They provide an assessment of the child/adolescent's peer acceptance, social competency and skills deficits (PRE forms) and also permit the evaluation of the effectiveness of the intervention programme in relation to areas previously assessed (POST, REVIEW forms).

Questions regarding social behaviour (What the child is like?) are included on rating scales completed by parent, teacher and child/adolescent self. The scales selected for inclusion represent the most commonly used criteria for referral of children and adolescents to the social skills training programme.

The scales measure:—

> peer acceptance/likability
> attention seeking behaviour
> aggressiveness (verbal and physical)
> self-confidence
> ability to cope with teasing
> maturity
> ability to make and keep friends.

A question regarding learning difficulties is included to give an indication of the ability of the child to cope with the cognitive or academic demands of the programme.

These rating scales are also used to evaluate change over the group term and review period for each individual child. The 5 point scale allows for trends to be detected over time. It also permits a comparison of relative social strengths and weaknesses from various significant viewpoints. Additional questions are included to provide a formal summary of goal identification (PRE GROUP), goal achievement (POST GROUP) and goal maintenance (REVIEW) for group participants.

To obtain a measure of the child's peer acceptance in the natural environment. (Is the child liked?), sociometric ratings are obtained from the child's school peers. The questions included on the peer rating scales, commonly used in sociometric ratings (Hymel and Asher, 1977; Sabornie and Ellis, 1987) are as follows:—

1. "How much do you play with ____?" is included to provide an indication of frequency of peer interaction in the school setting.

2. "How much do you like ____?" provides an indication of the child's likability by peers and may also be compared with the parent, teacher and self ratings of peer acceptability/likability (Question 1 on Parent, Teacher and Self Report Forms).

3. "Is ____ your friend?" is included to reflect the emphasis in the training programme on the acquisition of social skills (e.g. friendly approach behaviours) as pre-requisites for making and keeping friends. The peer ratings on this question may also be compared with teacher, parent and self reports regarding the child's ability to make and keep friends (Questions 8, 9 on Teacher, Parent Forms; Questions 5, 6 on Self Report Forms).

Thus a variety of measures are used to obtain a broad sampling of opinions regarding each child's specific skills and attributes and their development following intervention.

BEHAVIOUR MANAGEMENT COMPONENT

The issue of behavioural control of group members needs to be addressed if the group is to run smoothly and effectively. Many of the children referred for social training also behave disruptively. The following behaviour management methods are suitable.

Limit Setting

Rules for behaviour are suggested by the group leaders and may be modified by negotiation to suit the particular needs of the group.

These usually include

- one person speaks at a time
- everyone must listen
- no hurting others
- no damaging property
- if anyone becomes too excited or noisy or otherwise distracts the group, they will be asked to settle down.

Consequences of breaking these rules are generally determined by the group members, and may include time out from playtime or desirable group activities.

Problem Solving

Leaders may present the disruptive behaviour as a problem situation for group discussion. When the concentration of group members and the presentation of the formal section of the programme is interrupted, leaders may raise the issue of unfairness to them and other group members who may wish to contribute.

The STOP-THINK-DO principle is applied to solve this problem, with all members including the offender(s) being encouraged to give alternative solutions. A consensus decision is made on how the offending behaviour will be managed. Since this process takes time and interrupts the teaching of the formal lesson of the day, play time is reduced. Realizing this, children often apply pressure on offenders to modify their behaviour on subsequent occasions. The expression of a 'group feeling' regarding the consequences of disorderly behaviour (e.g. the postponement of playtime or a desired activity) is often a powerful management tool.

Goal Setting

Early in the group, children identify specific goals they would like to achieve. As they get to know the other members of the group, they also identify social goals for each other, e.g. children are asked, "I would like Paul better if ....." or "Debbie would be a better friend if ......" Their answers might include, "listen to others", "speak up," "not be so rough", "not whinge", "not boss", "behave more maturely", "share more", "not sulk".

These responses then become the child/adolescent's social goals in the group context (group goals) and are actively reinforced in the group sessions by social praise and/or stickers, points. Behaviour problems are thereby made manageable by the intermittent reinforcement of incompatible behaviours, which are usually identified in the process of goal setting.

FREE PLAY COMPONENT

Children in the 7 — 12 year groups are given the opportunity for free play for approximately 20 minutes of each weekly session. The playroom or an outside setting may be utilized. The children choose activities with the materials provided. The leaders are active participants in the play session, ensuring early intervention into potential problem situations. This requires vigilance on the part of the leaders and close co-operation so that the load of often rather exhausting intervention is shared between leaders. Following is a suggested dialogue for leaders when children are in conflict.

Approach the children involved in the situation. Say,
"Let's stop a minute!"
"What is happening here?"
"What is the problem?"

Encourage both children to look to each other and each to give their view of the problem. Ask both children,
"How do you feel about what happened?"
or, if more appropriate, ask one child,
"How would you feel if that happened to you?" Ask each child,
"What do you want to happen?"

In the early sessions before the problem solving method has been formally introduced, model the problem solving approach by saying,
"Let's find a way to make you both feel better."
Offer ideas along with the children.

After the STOP-THINK-DO problem solving method has been introduced (in session 4.) the above dialogue is expanded. The children are urged to produce their own solutions to the problem. Ask,
"What can you do to solve the problem?"
Elicit alternative solutions from each child involved, and also others in the group. In response to each solution offered, ask,
"What would happen if you did that?"

This encourages the children to examine the consequences of their solutions. Ask the children involved in the conflict,
"How would that make you feel?", referring to the consequences discussed.

Finally, encourage a choice of the best solution i.e. the one with the most acceptable consequences to both parties, making them both feel okay. Then, the thinking process must be followed by action. Add,
"It seems you both agree on that solution. Give it a try!"

If the solution works, reinforce both parties for their *"good thinking"* and skill at putting it into practice. Following playtime, discuss the problem solving exercise as a group.

If the conflict is not resolved, the leader mediates in the same manner outlined above adding,
"If that solution didn't work this time, there is always another one to try. Let's STOP and THINK of something else to DO."

Chapters 3, 4, 5 and 6 present the detailed, session by session content of programmes incorporating the major components presented in the overview.

Chapter 3
Social Skills
Training Programme
for Children 7 — 12 years

Chapter 3:
Social Skills Training Programme
For Children Aged 7 - 12 Years

OUTLINE

SOCIAL SKILLS TRAINING PROGRAMME FOR 7 — 12 YEAR OLDS
SESSION 1: GETTING TO KNOW YOU

Aims of Session 1

- to learn how to meet new people.
- to identify each child's social motivation in terms of their goals for group attendance.
- to get to know more about each other, the similarities and differences.
- to encourage group identity and trust between members.
- to establish rules for behaviour in the group.
- to encourage regular attendance.

Materials Required

- individual tags with name of each child and leader to be used in the first few weeks.
- Self Report Forms: PRE GROUP (Appendix 12) and pens.
- group rules displayed on poster for use each week.
- attendance chart with name of each child and 9 columns for recording attendance and homework completion each week.
- exercise book for each child in which is fixed homework for the first session.
- for Body Image activity
  — large sheet of paper for each child fixed to walls in the group room at just above head height.
  — textas
- for Blindfold Game
  — large handkerchiefs for use as blindfolds
- stickers for reinforcement of appropriate interpersonal behaviour.
- toys and activities for play session.

Procedure

1. Children are welcomed to group and asked to sit in a circle.
2. Self Report Forms: PRE GROUP completed by children. Explain and discuss each question, particularly the reference to goal identification.
3. Meeting People

   Name tags are placed face down in centre of circle. Leader chooses one tag and finds out to whom it belongs by asking:—
   "Is your name ....?"

   When the child is identified by name, find out more about them by asking questions such as:—
   "How old are you?"

   "What school do you go to?"

   "What things do you like to do?"

   "What is your favourite TV programme?"

The identified child then selects another name tag and repeats the above procedure with aid of leaders if necessary.

4. While introductions are proceeding, introduce the concept of 'same — different' by recognizing the similarities and differences in the children present. Emphasize that it is okay for people to be different and like different things — it makes meeting people interesting.

5. Following the introductions, discuss the rules for meeting people for the first time
   — approach them face to face
   — look at their eyes
   — smile and say hello
   — ask them questions about themselves
   — listen to them

6. Personal Goals

   Ask each child why they are attending the group and what they would like to achieve by participating in the programme. Record answers for future reference. Discuss similarities and differences in their reasons and goals.

7. Group Rules

   Discuss why we need rules in groups — so that everyone has a fair go.

   Rules (on poster) may include
   — only one person speaks at a time
   — everyone else must listen
   — everyone has a chance to speak if they want to
   — no hurting each other or the playroom
   — if anyone gets too excited, rough or noisy they will be asked to settle down.

   Discuss penalties for breaking the rules since the whole group suffers from disruptive behaviour which prevents effective group functioning. Encourage all children to contribute ideas about penalties and to take on the responsibility of reminding each other about the rules and penalties if necessary.

8. Alternative Activities To Get To Know Each Other
   - Body Image

     Children form pairs. One partner stands with his/her back against a sheet of paper on the wall while the other draws around his/her body. They change places on another sheet. Both then fill in the physical details of their partner (e.g. facial features, clothes). Encourage careful looking and asking questions between partners.

   - Blindfold Game

     Children form pairs. One of each pair is blindfolded. Pairs stand together at one end of room. Obstacles are placed in the room on the floor (e.g. upturned chairs, boxes, toys). Children must physically lead their blindfolded mates safely across the room without saying anything. Each pair then exchanges the blindfold. This time, children must guide their blindfolded partners through the obstacle course to the other side of the room by using only verbal directions and cues but no physical contact. The aim of the activity is to promote trust and co-operation. It is also an exercise to encourage careful listening and looking skills which are the topic for next session.

27

9. Play Session

    Children choose activities. Leaders participate and observe social interactions and model appropriate social skills. At this early stage in the group, if problems arise, urge children to stop what they are doing, say what the problem is while looking at and listening to the other child or children.

    Provide feedback about their behaviour during playtime.

10. Encourage Regular Commitment

    Explain the need for regular weekly attendance and completion of homework. Children earn 1 point for attending and 1 point for homework per week, which are recorded on the attendance chart. Record points for session 1 attendance. When children earn a certain number of points, (e.g. 6) they are eligible for a present from the lucky dip box at the end of session 4. If regular attendance and homework effort is maintained, the child receives another reward at the final session.

11. Homework

    Present each child with their homework book with session 1 homework, "Getting To Know Someone" affixed.

    Children are set an exercise which requires them to find out more about someone by looking more closely at them and/or asking questions.

12. Collect name tags before saying goodbye.

13. Pre Group Teacher Involvement

    Following this session, group leaders initiate first contact (termed PRE GROUP) with the teachers of the children whose parents have given permission.

    School peer acceptance of the children in the group is also assessed early in the training intervention (See Chapter 6).

Homework: Session 1 (for younger children)

GETTING TO KNOW YOU

Make this person look like your brother or sister or friend.

What is his/her name? _____

How old is he/she? _____

Homework: Session 1
GETTING TO KNOW SOMEONE

Ask your brother or sister the following questions and write down their answers.

1. How old are you?

    _____

2. What is your favourite food?

    _____

3. What food don't you like?

    _____

4. What is your favourite T.V. programme?

    _____

5. What games do you like to play?

    _____

Ask your friends at school the following questions and write down their answers.

1. How old are you?

    _____

2. Who is your favourite T.V. star?

    _____

2. What pets do you have?

    _____

4. What is your favourite sport?

    _____

5. What do you like to do after school?

    _____

GETTING TO KNOW SOMEONE

Ask your friends at school the following questions and write down their answers.

1. How old are you?

    _____

2. Do you have brothers or sisters?

    _____

3. What is your favourite sport and which team do you barrack for?

    _____

4. What did you do on the weekend?

    _____

5. What is your favourite T.V. programme?

    _____

6. What pop singer or group do you like to listen to?

    _____

7. What is your hardest subject at school?

    _____

8. What pets do you have?

    _____

9. Think of some other questions you could ask your friend.

    _____

    _____

    _____

SESSION 2: LOOKING AND LISTENING: BASIC SOCIAL SKILLS

Aims of Session 2

- to encourage the children to look carefully at others and listen to others to find out more about them.
- to teach feeling recognition by the LOOK and LISTEN method.
- to demonstrate feeling expression through body gestures, facial expressions and voice tone.
- to emphasize that different people can feel differently in the same situation.

Materials Required

- name tags, group rules poster, attendance chart, stickers, textas, toys (as per last session)
- for Reporter Game
  - interesting picture depicting action
  - 3 reporter "badges"
- for Detective Game
  - trench coat and hat
  - detective badge with "Inspector Gadget" for young ones, "Magnum" or "Sherlock Holmes" for older ones.
  - piece of jewellery to be hidden on the "thief"
- for Clancy the Clown story
  - large clown figure e.g. made from stockings stuffed with material and dressed appropriately
  - 4 interchangeable material faces depicting sad, happy, scared, angry feelings. The faces need to be easy to fix and remove. (Appendix 21)
  - toy dog
- homework for Session 2 to be affixed during the session.

Procedure

1. Review last session and homework exercise.
   - rules for meeting people
   - getting to know someone by looking at them and asking questions
   - group rules
2. Record points for attendance and homework completion on chart.
3. Alternative activities for practicing looking and listening skills.
   - Reporter Game

     Three children are chosen as reporters from various newspapers. They are instructed to wait outside of the room until called. The remaining children are shown an interesting picture and asked to describe what is happening in the picture. From these impressions, compose a 3-4 part story, with the complexity depending on the age of the children in the group. One child is elected to be the "eye-witness". A reporter is called in from outside the room and the eye witness recounts the story

32

from memory since the picture is now removed. A second reporter is called in and is told the story by the first reporter. Similarly, the third reporter is called in and told the story by the second reporter. The final version is usually quite different from the original. The reporters are finally shown the picture to discern these differences. Reinforce any examples of "good listening" in the reporters. The aim is to demonstrate how messages become distorted and misunderstood if we are not listening carefully and actively looking for clues.

- The Whispering Game

   Older children may enjoy a similar activity to the Reporter Game by forming a circle and passing a whispered message from person to person around the group. See how the message is misheard by careless listening and poor attention to details.

- The Detective Game

   One child is chosen to be detective, dons a coat, hat and badge, and leaves the room. Another child is chosen as the thief and given the jewellery to hide in a pocket. The other children look carefully at the thief and describe him/her. They must be able to answer the detective's questions correctly, but without giving away the identity of the thief by looking at him/her. The detective is called in and stands in the centre of the circle. He/she asks each child one question which must only be answered "yes" or "no". (e.g. Has the thief black hair? Is the thief wearing jeans?) Leaders encourage the detective to listen carefully to each clue and look carefully at each child to match the clues in order to identify the thief by the process of elimination.

4. Feeling Recognition and Expression

   Looking and listening skills also help us recognize **feelings** in other people. The Clancy the Clown play for younger children, and the Skateboard Story for older children illustrate feeling recognition and expression.

- Clancy the Clown Play

   The following feelings are illustrated using this puppet and mime — happy, worried, sad, surprised, scared, terrified, annoyed, mad, angry.

   Leader acts out the story holding the large puppet in front of him/her, showing the relevant actions and gestures, and altering the faces when appropriate. Alternatively, one leader may speak while the other leader mimes as directed.

   "Here is Clancy the Clown. He is walking along the street eating his favourite ice-cream. He feels very happy. *(Place 'happy' face on Clancy.)*How can we tell?

   > We look at his body — he is bouncing along with his shoulders back and his head held high.
   > We look at his face — his mouth is smiling and his eyes are bright and cheerful.
   > We listen to him — he might be singing or laughing.

   Can you look happy like Clancy? *(Demonstrate — children show each other).*

   Now, Clancy has finished his ice-cream. He has walked a long way and suddenly he realizes that he cannot remember which street he should take to get to his home. He starts to worry and feels very sad. *(Change Clancy's face to 'sad').* How can we tell?

   > We look at his body — he is slouching over and walking slowly with his shoulders hunched and head down.
   > We look at his face — his mouth is down in the corners, his eyes are half closed and might have tears in them. His chin might be quivering.

We listen to him — he might be sighing or even sobbing.

Can we look sad like Clancy? *(Demonstrate).*

Poor Clancy! But wait a minute! Here comes his little dog Snoopy running to meet him. What a pleasant surprise!

Snoopy will know the way home. Hooray! Clancy starts to feel happy again as he hugs his little pet. *(Place 'happy' face on Clancy and review How Can We Tell? Demonstrate).*

They're nearly home now. But around the corner comes Bill the Bully. He always likes to scare Clancy. He has often hurt Clancy and then says that he will do it again if Clancy dobs on him. Clancy is terrified. *(Change face to 'scared').* How can we tell?

> We look at his body — he is shaking and hiding his face behind his hands. He is stepping backwards.

> We look at his face — his mouth is open and trembling, his eyes are wide open and staring.

> We listen to him — he might say "please don't hurt me" or he might cry because he's scared.

Can you look scared like Clancy? *(Demonstrate).*

But today, Bill goes past Clancy and starts to pick on Snoopy. He even throws stones at him! Now, nothing makes Clancy more mad than someone picking on his dog. He is really angry. *(Change Clancy's face to 'angry').* How can we tell?

> We look at his body — he is standing straight with his feet spread apart, his fists clenched.

> We look at his face — his lips are held tightly together. His eyes look wild and he has a frown on his face.

> We listen to him — he might be gritting his teeth together, breathing heavily or even yelling.

Can you look angry like Clancy? *(Demonstrate).*

But, although Clancy feels angry, he decides that he won't get into a fight with Bill because he will probably get hurt. So, he picks up Snoopy and runs home.

What do we learn from this story?

— people like Clancy can feel different things at different times, one minute happy, the next sad or angry.

— we can find out how people feel by looking at them (body and face, especially mouth and eyes) and by listening carefully to them.

— different people can feel differently about something e.g. when Bill was throwing stones at Snoopy, he felt happy and powerful. Clancy felt quite differently — he was mad."

- The Skateboard Story

    The following feelings are illustrated using this story:— happy, surprised, excited, mad, scared, proud, terrified, bored, sad, worried, disappointed, annoyed, embarrassed, upset.

    Leader A is Ben, Leader B is his sister Emily. Each mimes appropriate actions and expressions as directed by the other leader who is the story teller at that time. The fewer the props, the more the actions, gestures and expressions are highlighted.

LEADER B speaks
LEADER A mimes

"This is Ben. He has just woken up and it is the morning of his birthday. He sees his present wrapped up at the end of his bed. He wonders what it is. He's feeling quite excited as he tears the paper off quickly. Wow! What a surprise! He had wished for a skateboard but didn't think he would get one. He feels really happy and runs to show his sister. How can we tell he is happy?

> We look at his body — he is bouncing along with his head held high and his shoulders back.

> We look at his face — his mouth is smiling and his eyes are bright and sparkling.

> We listen to him — he might be laughing or speaking in a pleasant voice. (Leader A laughs and calls out excitedly).

Ben and his sister Emily dress quickly and race down to the supermarket carpark to try out the new skateboard. As they turn the corner near their house, Greg, the neighbourhood tough guy comes toward them with a mean look on his face. He grabs the skateboard from under Ben's arm and threatens to break it over Emily's head.

LEADER A speaks
LEADER B mimes

Emily screams. She is so scared. In fact, she is terrified. How can we tell she feels scared?

> We look at her body — she is shaking and hiding her face behind her hands. She is stepping backwards behind her brother.

> We look at her face — her mouth is open and trembling, her eyes are wide open and staring.

> We listen to her as she might be screaming and crying out. (Leader B screams and cries out "don't hurt me").

LEADER B speaks
LEADER A mimes

Well Ben is not scared at all. He is feeling really angry about what Greg is doing to his new skateboard and his sister. He marches up to Greg who has put the board down and is ready to ride it. How can we tell Ben is feeling mad?

> We look at his body — he is standing straight with his feet spread apart, his fists are clenched and he is stepping forward.

> We look at his face — his lips are held tightly together. His eyes look wild and he has a frown on his face.

> We listen to him — he might be gritting his teeth together, breathing heavily or even yelling. (Leader A breathes heavily).

But, even though Ben feels really angry, he stops for a second and thinks about how getting into a fight might lead to more trouble or someone getting hurt on his birthday. So, he quickly grabs Emily's hand and picks up his skateboard and runs off as fast as he can.

They reach the supermarket carpark. Ben is riding fast across the cement, zig-zagging between the lines like a real star. He feels happy again.

LEADER A speaks
LEADER B mimes

But not so Emily. She is thoroughly bored, sitting on the footpath waiting for her brother to finish so she can go home. (Instruct the children to show how they look when they feel bored like Emily). Finally she asks Ben for a turn. Well, it is her first try at riding a skateboard, and it keeps sliding out from under her feet. She feels rather scared. She also feels embarrassed because Ben keeps laughing at her. Fortunately, this only makes her more determined. She keeps on trying until finally, she is able to skateboard down the hill with no problems. Does she feel proud of herself! Show me how you look when you're feeling proud of yourself.

LEADER B speaks
LEADER A mimes

Now it is Ben's turn again. But Oh, No! One of the wheels is stuck in the gutter grating. He tries to pull it out but he is bending the axle. He feels so disappointed. His new skateboard — broken! He slumps down in the gutter feeling very sad. How can we tell?

> We look at his body — he is slouching over with his head down.

> We look at his face — his mouth is down at the corners, his eyes are half-closed and might have tears in them. His chin might be quivering.

> We listen to him — he might be sighing, or even sobbing. (Leader A sighs heavily and says sadly "Oh, No!").

Although he is really upset, he stops and thinks about how he could work this problem out. He has an idea! Emily pushes down the grating while he slides the wheel out. It works! And nothing is really broken.

Ben and Emily feel happy as they run home to enjoy the rest of Ben's birthday.

What do we learn from this story?

— people can feel different things at different times, one minute happy, the next sad or angry.

— we can find out how people feel by looking at them (body and face, especially mouth and eyes) and by listening carefully to them.

— different people can feel differently about something e.g. when Greg the tough guy was threatening Emily, he felt strong and powerful. Emily felt quite differently — she was scared. Ben felt differently again — he was angry.

5. Play Session

Discuss the feelings which are displayed during play. Encourage children to look carefully at and listen carefully to other children so that they can pick up the cues for feelings in body and facial gestures, and voice tone.

6. Homework

The children are given a job as a detective to find out more about others, including their feelings.

7. Leaders' Meeting

Leaders from both child and parent groups meet following this session for a discussion re:

- the parents' views of their children's problems and goals for the children and themselves.

- teachers' views of the children's problems and goals for the children.

- the leaders' views of the children from observations in the group sessions.

- the children's goals for themselves.

On the basis of this discussion, individual goals are determined for each child which will be reinforced in the group sessions for both children and parents, and will be discussed at the teacher training session following Session 3.

LOOKING AND LISTENING: BASIC SOCIAL SKILLS

You are a detective. Find a picture of someone who is feeling happy and stick it in your homework book.

How can you tell that they are happy?

_____

_____

Now, find a picture of someone who is feeling sad and stick it in.

How can you tell that they are sad?

_____

_____

Finally, find a picture of someone who is feeling mad and stick it in.

How can you tell that they feel mad?

_____

_____

Homework: Session 2 (for older children)

LOOKING AND LISTENING: BASIC SOCIAL SKILLS

You are a detective. Find out how these people are feeling by looking carefully at their face and actions, and by listening to them.

1. How does your mum feel when you won't eat the dinner she has cooked?

    _____

    _____

2. How does your dad feel when his football team wins?

    _____

    _____

3. How did you feel when you first came to this group?

    _____

    _____

4. How does your friend feel when he/she gets teased.

    _____

    _____

5. What makes your brother or sister scared?

    _____

    _____

6. How can you make your friend feel happy?

    _____

    _____

SESSION 3: LOOKING AND LISTENING: BASIC SOCIAL SKILLS

Aims of Session 3
- to identify a broad range of feelings for recognition and expression.
- to encourage the appreciation of causes or reasons for feelings.
  "Why does she feel like that? Because .... happened."
- to discuss ways of making people feel better.
- to identify prosocial goals for each child to be achieved through personal feedback and reinforcement within the supportive group.

Materials Required
- group rules poster, attendance chart, stickers, textas, paper, toys.
- for Charades Game
  - large empty tissue box called the 'Feeling Box' which has a hole in top to fit hand.
  - cards with a feeling situation described on each.

  Examples for Feeling Box

  Child is sitting in class drawing carefully, and neighbour leans over and scribbles on the picture.

  Child opens maths test which teacher has just marked and handed back. Child has failed the test.

  Child is walking through the door at home and brother trips him/her.

  Child has bought an ice cream and is just about to eat it when it drops on the ground.

  Child is helping mother with the dinner dishes and drops mother's best dinner plate.

  Children are playing ball. Another child wants to join but is ignored.

  Child is playing football/netball and scores the winning goal for the team.

  Child is having a picnic in the scrub, turns over a rock to sit on and sees a big lizard.
- for Feeling Wheel

  a free spinning wheel about ¾ metre diameter made from a board with a pivot and marker in the centre. The surface of the wheel is divided into a number of segments, each marked with a different feeling word e.g. happy, sad, worried, bored, annoyed, disappointed, scared, embarrassed, mad, surprised.
- for Story Time

  a book suitable for younger children depicting various feelings as part of the story (e.g. Little Golden Book, "Petey and I"
  by M.O.Conn, 1973, Golden Press; Sydney).
- for Feelings Collage

  magazines, scissors, paste, large sheet of cardboard or paper, textas.
- homework for session 3 to be affixed during the session.

Procedure

1. Review last session and homework exercise.
   - finding out more about people by looking at them and listening carefully.
   - recognizing feelings using the same skills.
   - being a detective on the trail of feelings for homework.

2. Record points for attendance and homework completion on chart.

3. Alternative activities for practicing feeling recognition and identifying reasons for feelings. "Why does he/she feel ....? Because .... happened."

   - Charades

     Children are divided into two groups, each with an adult.

     One group chooses a leader who draws a card from the Feeling Box and organizes the charade. The group must silently act out the feeling situation described, showing appropriate facial and body gestures. The other group watches carefully and then discusses **what** is happening and **how** the children are feeling and **why** they are feeling that way. They must co-operate and reach a consensus opinion on these questions to put to the first group. Points may be allotted. The groups then reverse roles for another charade drawn from the Feeling Box.

   - Feeling Wheel

     Children take turns spinning the wheel. When it stops on a feeling word, the child is asked about the feeling:—

     Have you ever felt like that?

     Show us how you looked when you felt like that.

     (Children may also look at themselves in the one-way screen if available).

     Why did you feel like that?

     What did you do about it to make you feel better? (if appropriate).

   - Story Time (for younger children)

     Leader reads a story depicting a number of different feelings in various interpersonal situations. Encourage children to examine the pictures for feeling clues — facial expressions, body gestures, actions, and to listen to the tone of the voice used to describe the feelings and the situations that caused them. Whenever a feeling is described, stop and ask the children the same questions as for the Feeling Wheel activity.

   - Feelings Collage (for younger children)

     Children look through magazines and cut out pictures displaying different feelings. A big sheet of paper is laid on the floor and divided into sections marked with feeling words (happy, sad, mad, scared, shy). Children then match the picture with the corresponding feeling word. Encourage the children to seek opinions from other members of the group as to why the people in the pictures are feeling like they are, before they paste it on the collage. It is then a co-operative group product and may be fixed on the wall for reference in following sessions.

4. Personal Feedback

   Leader writes each child's name on a separate sheet of paper divided into two sections. Ask the children to say what they like about each child and record the answers on one section of paper. Then ask what they would like the child to do more often, and record on the other section. Encourage the children to be specific e.g.

"Michael is friendly and fun to play with and..."

"We would like him to listen more to others and to ask for things rather than take them and..."

or

"Sarah is helpful and well behaved and..."

"We would like her to look at the person when she speaks and use a louder voice and..."

These suggestions then become the group goals for each child and should be left on the walls of the group room. Children are asked to notice when others are trying to achieve their goals. Leaders should reinforce these during following sessions with positive comments, stickers. Information regarding these goals are fed back to parents and also teachers to follow up in their respective settings.

5. Play Session

    Focus further on feeling recognition during play time. Encourage children to say why they (or others) feel that way and also how they could make themselves or others feel better.

6. Preparations for Teacher Training Session

    Advise the group of the teachers' meeting following this session. Record the responses of each person to the questions:—

    "What do you think your teacher will say about you?"

    "What would he/she want you to achieve by attending the group?"

    These comments are useful to discuss with teachers.

7. Homework

    Children identify various feelings and reasons why people feel like that and what could be done to make them feel better.

RECOGNIZING AND EXPRESSING FEELINGS

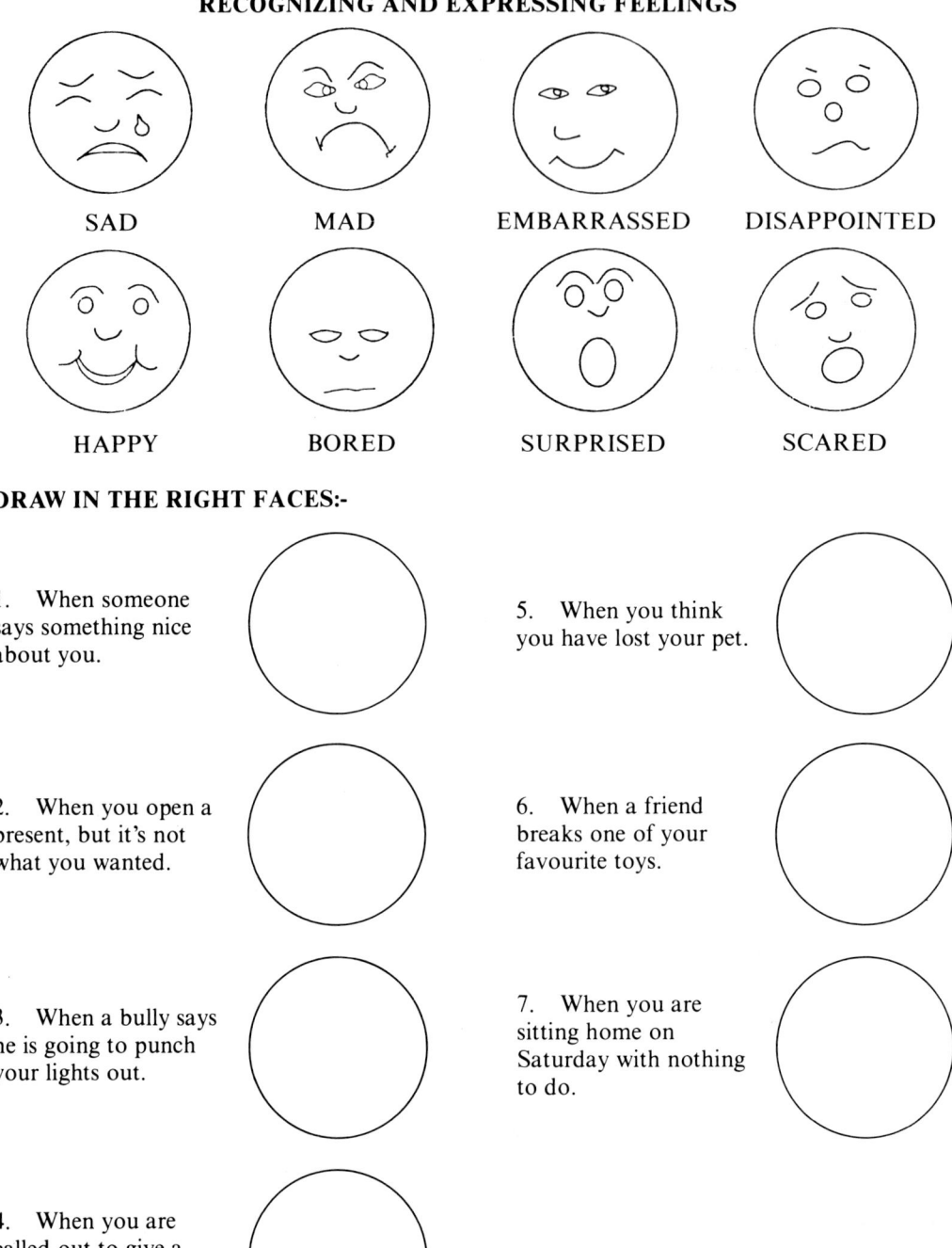

SAD   MAD   EMBARRASSED   DISAPPOINTED

HAPPY   BORED   SURPRISED   SCARED

DRAW IN THE RIGHT FACES:-

1. When someone says something nice about you.

2. When you open a present, but it's not what you wanted.

3. When a bully says he is going to punch your lights out.

4. When you are called out to give a talk in front of the class.

5. When you think you have lost your pet.

6. When a friend breaks one of your favourite toys.

7. When you are sitting home on Saturday with nothing to do.

RECOGNIZING AND EXPRESSING FEELINGS

Feeling	Find a Picture to Show the Feeling	Why Do You Think They Feel Like That?	What Can You Do To Make Them Feel Better?
Happy			
Sad			
Mad			
Scared			

RECOGNIZING AND EXPRESSING FEELINGS

(A piece of cardboard 20 cm square and a pivot pin are provided).

Make your own Feeling Wheel at home. Cut out a circle and divide it into 8 different segments. Colour the segments different colours and write a different feeling word on each (see example below). Cut out a cardboard pointer, and join it to a pivot pin through the centre of the wheel. Ask your parents, brothers, sisters, friends or relatives to spin the pointer to select a feeling. Then ask them these questions about the feeling:—

"Have you ever felt like that?"

"Why did you feel like that?"

"What would make you feel better?"

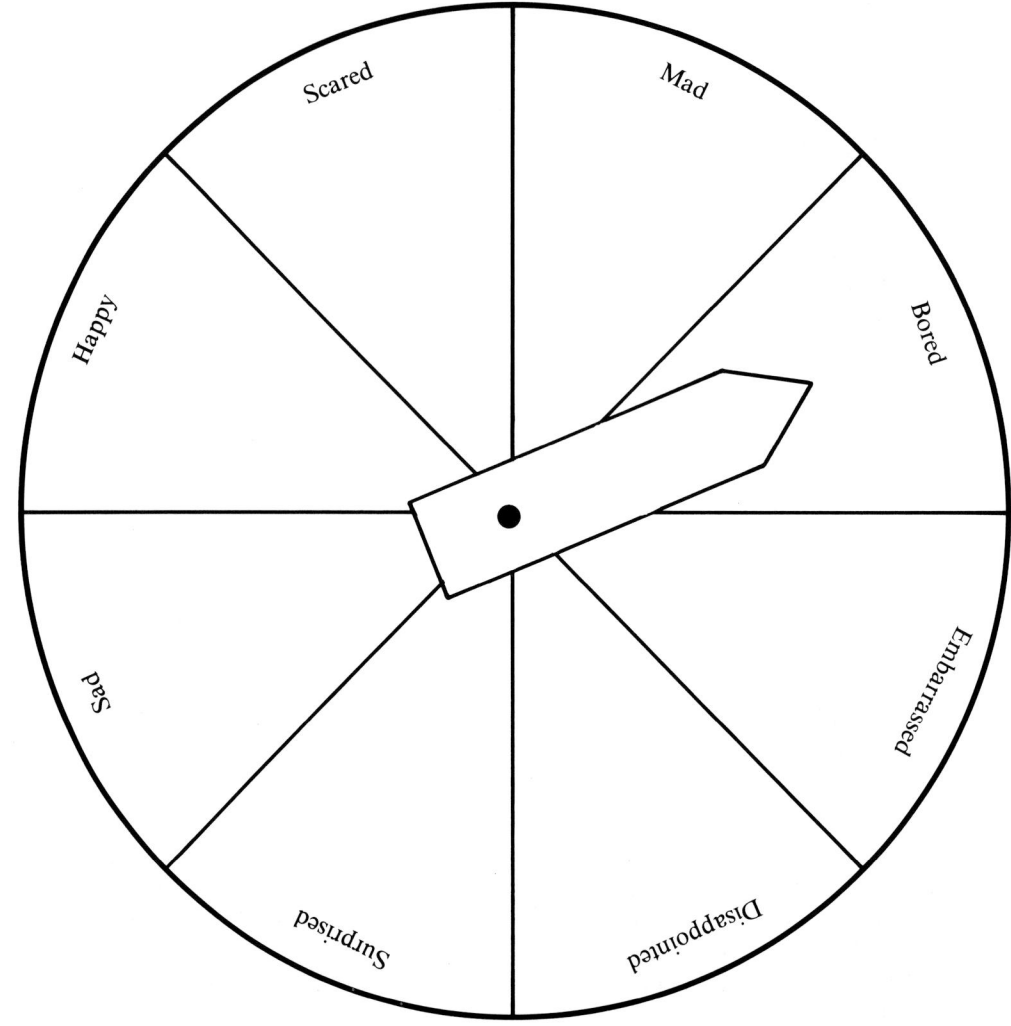

SESSION 4: SOLVING SOCIAL PROBLEMS WITH STOP-THINK-DO.

Aims of Session 4

- to teach the STOP-THINK-DO step by step approach for solving social problems using the traffic light motto.

STOP (red)	— define problem
	— recognize feelings
	— identify goals
THINK (yellow)	— generate solutions
	— evaluate consequences
DO (green)	— choose solution
	— initiate action

Materials Required

- attendance chart, stickers, textas, paper, toys
- group goal sheets completed last week to be displayed on walls
- STOP-THINK-DO posters (Appendix 18)
- video recorder and monitor
- video of "The New Girl" from "What Should I Do?" series (Additional Resource Materials). If video is unavailable, a social interaction problem situation may be described or roleplayed (see homework exercises)
- for STOP-THINK-DO badges
  - black cardboard
  - red, yellow, green adhesive circles
  - scissors, safety pins, sticky tape
- homework for session 4 to be affixed during the session
- rewards for children to choose

Procedure

1. Review last session and homework exercise.
   - recognizing feelings — How can we tell?
   - reasons for feelings — Why ...... because......?
   - handling feelings — What makes us feel better? Introduce the idea that there are many different ways of making people feel better. These are alternative solutions.
2. Record points for attendance and homework completion on chart.
3. Group Goals

   Draw children's attention to the feedback they received from each other last session about possible ways to improve their behaviour and develop more skills. Encourage children to try out the suggestions and reinforce each other's efforts. Leaders do the same with comments, stickers.

   Discuss the goals also in the light of teachers' comments from the Teacher Training Session.

4. STOP-THINK-DO Approach to Problem Solving

Some parents may participate for this section.

Instruct the children to close their eyes and imagine the following situation:—
"You have just changed schools. You don't know many people at your new school. You want to join in a game with some children at recess time, but you're not sure if they will let you.

Let me show you a video about a girl in just this position and see how she tried to solve her problem to make herself feel better."

Show video of "The New Girl" or describe/roleplay a social interaction problem situation which raises questions such as:—

How can you meet people and make friends when you're new to a school?

Who can you talk to if you do not have friends yet?

How can you make people notice you without being a show off?

What if you look different or dress differently from the others?

- Point to red light on traffic light motto.

"Let's STOP right there!"

"Look at the problem before you rush into anything."

"What is happening here?"

"How does she feel?"

"How can you tell?"

Discuss her facial expressions, body posture, voice tone.

"How would you feel if you were in that situation?"

"What would you want to happen if you were her?"

Discuss the goals the children would have if they were in the same situation.

- Point to yellow light on traffic light motto.

"Now THINK"

"What could she do about it?"

"How would you solve the problem?"

Record the children's solutions encouraging as many alternatives as possible. Evaluate consequences of each answer. Ask,

"What might happen if she/you did that?" after each suggestion.

"How would she/you feel then?"

- Point to green light on traffic light motto.

"Which is the best solution to choose?"

"Which would make everyone feel better?"

"DO it!"

"If it doesn't work, try another solution. There is always an answer if we stop and think about it."

Parents return to their group at this point.

5. Traffic Light Badges

Children make their own traffic light badge to wear home to remind themselves of the STOP-THINK-DO way of solving problems. Encourage them to show parents, siblings, friends and discuss its significance.

6. Play Session

Leaders model the STOP-THINK-DO approach where specific conflict arises during playtime. Urge the children to follow the above sequence of steps.

7. Homework

An interpersonal conflict situation is presented for the children to solve using the STOP-THINK-DO approach. Younger children may ask parents to write their answers. A number of alternative exercises are provided which are suitable for practice in the sessions or for homework.

8. Rewards

Children may have accumulated enough points for a choice from the rewards box. Encourage continued regular attendance and homework completion.

SOLVING SOCIAL PROBLEMS WITH STOP-THINK-DO

Tom is playing with Jane in the sandpit. Jane throws sand at Tom and gets it in his eyes.

STOP: What is the problem?

_____

_____

How does Tom feel?

_____

_____

How does Jane feel?

_____

_____

THINK: What could Tom do?

1. _____

2. _____

3. _____

What could Jane do?

1. _____

2. _____

3. _____

DO: What is the best solution?

_____

_____

_____

SOLVING SOCIAL PROBLEMS WITH STOP-THINK-DO

STOP: What is the problem?
Mark just started to play with the pinball machine, and Stephen came over to him and took over the game.

How does Mark feel?

_____

_____

How does Stephen feel?

_____

_____

THINK: What might happen next?

1. _____

2. _____

3. _____

DO: What can they do so that they **both** feel OK?

_____

_____

_____

SOLVING SOCIAL PROBLEMS WITH STOP-THINK-DO

You are playing with a ball in the school yard when Paul snatches it off you.

STOP: What is the problem?

_____

_____

How do you feel?

_____

_____

How does Paul feel?

_____

_____

What do you want to happen?

_____

_____

THINK: of three (3) things you could do to solve the problem.

1. _____

2. _____

3. _____

DO: Which would you choose to do?

_____

_____

_____

SOLVING SOCIAL PROBLEMS WITH STOP-THINK-DO

You are watching your favourite TV programme and your brother/sister changes the channel without asking you.

STOP: What is the problem?

_____

_____

How do you feel?

_____

_____

How does your brother/sister feel?

_____

What do you want to happen?

_____

THINK: of three (3) things that you could do to solve the problem

1. _____

2. _____

3. _____

DO: Which would you choose to do?

_____

_____

SOLVING SOCIAL PROBLEMS WITH STOP-THINK-DO

A child at school keeps annoying you by bumping or pushing you as you pass.

1. How does the child feel?

    _____

    _____

2. How do you feel?

    _____

    _____

3. What do you want to happen?

    _____

    _____

4. What could you do about it?

    _____

    _____

5. How might the child feel then?

    _____

    _____

6. How might you feel then?

    _____

    _____

7. Is this a good idea?

    _____

    _____

8. Think of another idea.

    _____

    _____

9. How could you both feel better?

    _____

    _____

SESSION 5: SOLVING PROBLEMS THE COOL WAY

Aims of Session 5

- to teach the children to differentiate Cool, Weak and Aggro response styles

  COOL _____ politely assertive

  WEAK_____ passive

  AGGRO _____ aggressive.

- to encourage children to categorize solutions generated in the THINK step of the STOP-THINK-DO method according to the COOL/WEAK/AGGRO criteria.

- to emphasize that the COOL way of behaving often leads to the most acceptable consequences and is therefore useful to try first to solve social problems.

Materials Required

- attendance chart, STOP-THINK-DO posters, stickers, textas, paper.
- COOL/WEAK/AGGRO posters (Appendix 19)
- video recorder and monitor
- video of "The Fight" from "What Should I Do?" series.

  If video is unavailable, a social problem situation may be described or roleplayed (see homework exercises)

- video camera
- for STOP-THINK-DO collage

  — magazines

  — large red, yellow and green circles of card board about 1 metre in diameter

  — scissors, glue

- homework for Session 5 to be affixed during the session

Procedure

1. Review last session and homework exercises.

   — use posters to review STOP-THINK-DO approach to solving problems.

   — discuss conflict situation presented for homework. The solutions offered by children usually include:—

   using physical force (hitting, grabbing)

   using verbal force (yelling, abusing)

   crying, sulking

   telling someone else (parent, teacher.)

   asking or speaking nicely

   bargaining ("If you do that, I will do something for you")

   walking away, ignoring, doing something else.

2. Record points for attendance and homework completion on chart.

3. Introduce COOL/WEAK/AGGRO Ways of Behaving

Refer to homework exercise and the usual solutions as described above. Each of these solutions may be categorized as COOL (appropriately assertive), WEAK (passive) or AGGRO (aggressive).

- Choose a weak solution from the homework. Have some of the children roleplay the problem and the solution. Ask remaining children to describe how the person who is behaving in a weak way sounds and looks. Older children may respond well to videotaping the exercise and discussing it on playback. Refer to posters for verbal, non-verbal and emotional characteristics of a WEAK response.

The WEAK way is to:—

talk softly, mumble

cry or sulk when faced with a problem

look down at the floor

stand far away, hunched over

give in to others

feel shy, embarrassed, nervous, useless, unhappy

- Choose an aggro solution from the homework exercise. Roleplay the solution and children again describe how a person who is behaving in an aggro way looks and sounds. Refer to poster.

The AGGRO way is to:—

shout, yell

speak rudely, abuse, tease, put down

blame others

look mad

stand close and threaten

push, hit, kick

feel angry, annoyed, out of control

- Choose a cool solution from the homework exercise. Use a TV personality to exemplify cool behaviour (eg Fonzie in "Happy Days"). Roleplay the solution and children describe how cool behaviour looks and sounds. Refer to poster.

The COOL way is to:—

speak firmly but friendly

stand up for yourself politely

smile or look calm

stand tall

look other person in the eyes

feel happy, confident, in control, okay about yourself.

4. Problem Solving Video "The Fight"

Some parents may participate at this point.

Present the video as an example of a conflict situation. Divide the group into two with a parent and leader in each. Using traffic light motto, go through problem solving steps as in last session. Additionally, encourage children to describe their solutions in terms of COOL/WEAK/AGGRO criteria. Follow with a discussion of consequences of each behaviour and a choice of the best solution i.e. the one with the most acceptable consequences to all concerned. Emphasize that the COOL way often leads to the most acceptable consequences for the people concerned and is therefore often a good first choice solution.

5. Alternative Group Activities

    *   Stop-Think-Do Collage (for younger children)

        Children cut out pictures from magazines which depict conflict situations where negative feelings are being shown. These are pasted on the large red circle of cardboard reminding them to STOP when they have a problem. On the large yellow circle, pictures of people contemplating, thinking or planning are pasted, reminding them to THINK to find answers to conflicts. On the large green circle are pasted pictures of people in positive action, playing, co-operating, with happy expressions, reminding them to choose the best solution they can think of and DO it.

    *   Video Roleplay (older children)

        Following on from the video of "The Fight", children roleplay and video their choice of the best solution. Invite discussion regarding the advantages of COOL behaviour over other ways of solving conflicts.

6. Play Session

    Reinforce STOP-THINK-DO approach, especially utilizing COOL ways of conflict resolution.

7. Homework

    Children are given interpersonal problems and solutions to evaluate in terms of COOL/WEAK/AGGRO criteria.

8. Leaders' Meeting

    Following this session, leaders from child and parent groups meet to review progress and evaluate goals for each child and parent in the programme.

SOLVING SOCIAL PROBLEMS THE COOL WAY

1. Someone throws stones at you, so you get back at them by breaking their pencils.

   Is this AGGRO/COOL/WEAK? _____

   _____

   How could you have acted in a COOL way? _____

   _____

2. Other kids are being asked to join in a game, but no-one asks you. You stand there and say nothing and just feel sad.

   Is this COOL/AGGRO/WEAK? _____

   _____

   How could you have acted in a COOL way? _____

   _____

3. You are playing with a pinball game and your friend tries to push in. You tell him nicely that he can have a turn after you. Is this COOL/AGGRO/WEAK? _____

   _____

   How could you have acted in a COOL way? _____

   _____

4. Other kids tease you and call you "dumbo" because you're no good at schoolwork. You run and tell the teacher.

   Is this COOL/AGGRO/WEAK? _____

   _____

   How could you have acted in a COOL way? _____

   _____

Homework: Session 5 (for older children)
SOLVING PROBLEMS THE COOL WAY

Peter is in your class at school. He is clumsy at sport and not very good at his schoolwork. He gets called names like "Dumbo" and is not asked to join in games because he is too slow. He often sits by himself at lunch times.

1. **STOP:** What is the problem?

_____

_____

How does Peter feel?

_____

_____

How do you feel?

_____

What do you want to happen? _____

_____

2. **THINK:** What things can Peter do to solve his problem?

1. _____

   Is this COOL/WEAK/AGGRO? _____

2. _____

   Is this COOL/WEAK/AGGRO? _____

3. _____

   Is this COOL/WEAK/AGGRO? _____

What things can you do? _____

_____

3. DO: What is the best thing for Peter to do?

_____

Is that COOL/ WEAK/ AGGRO? _____

_____

4. Have you ever been teased? _____

What happened? _____

_____

What did you do? _____

What would be a COOL thing to do? _____

_____

We will talk more about teasing next session.

SOCIAL SKILLS TRAINING GROUP FOR 7 — 12 YEAR OLDS
SESSION 6: SOLVING PROBLEMS THE FRIENDLY WAY

Aims of Session 6

- to emphasize that to have friends you have to behave like one.
- to teach children to recognize friendly ways of behaving when solving social problems. FRIENDLY _____ fair, co-operative, considerate, respectful of others.
- to demonstrate that the FRIENDLY way is generally compatible with the COOL way.
- to instruct children in effective ways of handling unfriendly behaviour, especially teasing and put downs.
- to increase motivation for behaving in a friendly way by identifying and reinforcing prosocial goals for each child in the supportive group environment.

Materials Required

- attendance chart, stickers, textas, paper, STOP-THINK-DO and COOL/ WEAK/AGGRO posters, toys and materials for co-operative play (e.g. puppets, dress-up clothes, ball games)
- video recorder and monitor
- video "The Game" from "What Should I Do?" series. If video is unavailable, a social problem situation may be described or roleplayed (see homework exercises)
- video camera (if suitable)
- for Teasing Shield
    - cardboard boxes or pieces of thick cardboard for children to cut out shields
    - paints, water, brushes
    - elastic for hand grip made by punching two holes in shield about a hand width apart, threading elastic through and knotting
    - large sheet of plastic for floor protection (if necessary)
- homework for session 6 to be affixed during session.

Procedure

1. Review last session and homework exercise.
    - STOP-THINK-DO method of problem solving, following the traffic light motto as a reminder of the various steps.
    - COOL/WEAK/AGGRO ways of solving problems as shown in the homework exercises.
    - the COOL way is to look directly at others, speak firmly but positively, stand up for yourself politely, feel confident and okay.
2. Record points for attendance and homework completion on chart
3. Friendship Discussion

   Discuss the notion that to have a friend, you have to behave like one. Emphasize qualities like fairness, co-operation, consideration of others, trust, loyalty, kindness as components of friendship.

Divide into smaller groups , each with a leader. Pose these questions to the children —
"What is a friend?"

"What do you like about your friends?"

"What do you do with your friends?"

Record the children's answers to these questions on paper. Return to larger group. Leader writes each child's name on a large sheet of paper. The group is asked "How could ... be a better friend?" for each child. Record the suggestions. Also ask for ideas on how the children in the group can help each other to be a better friend. Fix the sheets to the wall for children and leaders to refer to during the session. Actively reinforce "friendly" behaviours.

4.   Problem Solving Video "The Game"

Parents may participate at this point.

Emphasize the need for fairness and co-operation in social interactions if conflicts are to be resolved 'in a friendly way'. Divide into two groups, each with a leader and parent. Encourage the children to think of alternative solutions to the problem situation depicted in the video (or situation described/roleplayed) which are both COOL and FRIENDLY. They will also see that AGGRO and WEAK solutions are often unfriendly in the sense that they do not lead to co-operation and fairness to all concerned.

5.   Roleplay

Children roleplay the alternative solutions suggested to the problem in the video and possible consequences of each solution. Older children may like to video these roleplays for playback and further discussion. Particularly emphasize the COOL and the FRIENDLY ways, and note the consequences of making people feel better. Friendship is based on such consequences: to be a friend is to be fair and considerate.

6.   Handling Unfriendly Behaviour

Discuss examples of people behaving in an unfriendly way toward each other. Refer also to video of "The Game" for examples, such as:—

> pushing in front of others
> refusing to let them join in play
> being physically rough
> cheating in games
> teasing

Refer to homework regarding the boy who was teased for being slow and dumb. Ask the children to recall times when they were teased, how they felt and how they reacted. Encourage them to think of other ways of handling teasing that might work better (e.g. walking away, laughing at the teasing).Another way that some children find useful involves the erection of an imaginary shield around them. Some children like to make the sound of the words bouncing off the shield and others imagine it has a particular colour or texture. The important point is that while children are THINKING about the shield, they are not paying attention to the teasing. They then have more time to think of an appropriate way to handle the situation rather than just react in their usual but often ineffective ways.

7.   The Teasing Shield

Children make and decorate a hand held shield. This is a symbol of their imaginary shield which they can "think up" anytime as a protection against teasing. Reinforce friendly, co-operative behaviour while shields are being made and decorated.

8. Play Session

Provide further opportunities for a co-operative activity involving a number of children at once e.g. puppet plays, collage making, team ball-games, drama. Reinforce friendly (i.e. fair, co-operative, kind) behaviour, especially when used to solve problems.

9. Homework

Exercises focus on being a friend and handling unfriendly behaviour.

Homework: Session 6 (for younger children)
SOLVING PROBLEMS THE FRIENDLY WAY

1. Draw your imaginary shield. What colour and shape is it?

2. Did your imaginary shield help you handle teasing this week? What happened? _____

_____

_____

_____

_____

Homework: Session 6 (for older children)
SOLVING PROBLEMS THE FRIENDLY WAY

1. Did your imaginary shield help you handle teasing this week?
   If yes, what happened?

   _____

   _____

   How did you feel after you used your shield? _____

   _____

2. What other ways help you handle teasing or put downs? _____

   _____

3. Has someone been a friend to you this week?
   If yes, what did they do or say? _____

   _____

   How did you feel? _____

   _____

4. Have you been a friend to someone this week?
   If yes, what did you do or say? _____

   _____

   How did you feel? _____

   _____

5. How could you be a better friend? _____

   _____

SESSION 7: SOLVING PROBLEMS THE RIGHT WAY

Aims of Session 7

- to demonstrate the pressures of friendship on our choices of solutions to social problems involving moral issues.

- to illustrate that, in some situations, we may not feel that the FRIENDLY way (the way our friends would like us to behave) is the RIGHT way (the way our parents/others have taught us) or even the COOL way (standing up appropriately for ourselves)

  RIGHT ———— responsible, moral, expected.

- to emphasize that such conflicts can be resolved through an evaluation of short and long term consequences of each course of action in each particular situation.

Materials Required

- attendance charts, stickers, textas, STOP-THINK-DO and COOL/WEAK/AGGRO posters, toys.

- video recorder and monitor.

- video of "The Lunch Money" from "What Should I Do?" series or description/roleplay of similar social problem situation.

- homework for session 7 is affixed during the session.

Procedure

1. Review last session and homework exercise.

   — how friends behave. Refer to homework exercise.

   — the FRIENDLY way to solve problems is with co-operation, fairness, consideration and respect for others.

   — how to handle unfriendly behaviour, especially teasing and put downs.

   Refer to homework exercise and discuss use of imaginary shield.

2. Record points for attendance and homework completion on chart.

3. The Pressures of Friendship

   Sometimes our friends put pressure on us to do something which we don't really agree with and feel is not right. It might be something that others like our parents wouldn't want us to do. Doing the responsible or right thing may not be what our friends want us to do, and we still want to keep our friends. So, we have conflict going on inside of us like the children in the following situations.

4. Moral Dilemmas

   Instruct the children to close their eyes and imagine the following situations. These may be roleplayed instead of using imagery.

   Situation 1: Richard and Andrew are good friends. They often play with a pinball machine at the local Deli. One day, Andrew went over to the counter to buy a drink. While the shop owner turned away to get the drink, Andrew took a Mars Bar and hid it under his jumper. He then paid for the drink and went back to Richard at the pinball machine. But Richard had seen his friend steal the Mars Bar.

Children open their eyes. Discuss the following using the STOP-THINK-DO procedure.

How does Richard feel?

How does Andrew feel?

What could Richard do? Is this COOL/WEAK/AGGRO?

What could Andrew do? Is this COOL/WEAK/AGGRO?

Is it a FRIENDLY thing to do?

What do you think is the RIGHT thing for each boy to do?

Children close their eyes again.

> Situation 2: Debbie and Craig are walking home from school. They pass an old house with a broken window. They don't know if anyone lives there. Craig picks up some stones and begins to throw them at the windows in the old house. Debbie doesn't like the idea. He says to her "Come on, don't be a chicken, don't be weak" and he hands her some stones to throw as well.

Children open eyes and discuss as with Situation 1. Possible solutions may include the use of an imaginary shield to protect against teasing from Craig if Debbie chooses to do what she thought was right.

> Situation 3: David and Sarah are playing around the local supermarket which is closed with a group of their friends on skateboards. There is a heap of rubbish piled against the wall outside of the supermarket. One of their friends lights up a match and suggests that they set a light to the rubbish next to the supermarket.

> Situation 4: Louise always finds maths hard. She sits next to Karen who is good at maths and often helps her with her work. But today is a maths test and the teacher has asked everyone to do their own work, but Louise can't do it. She leans over and tries to copy Karen's answers.

Open eyes and discuss as above.

5. Problem Solving Video "The Lunch Money"

Parents may participate at this point.

The moral dilemma presented in this video is similar to that portrayed in Situation 1. Following the video, divide into two groups to discuss according to the same procedure. With older children, encourage them to evaluate the short and long term consequences of each possible solution. Also, emphasize the pressures which friendship imposes when evaluating possible solutions and consequences. Sometimes we must weigh the friendship on one hand and doing what we think is the right thing on the other hand.

Sometimes the RIGHT way may NOT be the FRIENDLY way, at least in the short term.

Well, is it the COOL way?

Or can the RIGHT way be WEAK, or AGGRO?

Discuss according to the maturity of the children in the group.

6. Play Session

7. Homework

Moral dilemmas to solve.

8. Leaders' Meeting

Leaders of child and parent groups meet following this session to review goals and evaluate progress.

SOLVING PROBLEMS THE RIGHT WAY

Robert wants to join a special gang at school. The leader of the gang tells him that if he goes to the newsagent and steals a pen and rubber, he can join the gang. Robert *really* wants to be accepted into the group.

STOP: What is the problem?

_____

_____

How does Robert feel?

_____

_____

THINK: Name three (3) things that Robert could do.

1. He could _____

_____

2. He could _____

_____

3. He could _____

_____

DO: What do you think is the RIGHT thing to do?

_____

_____

Is that COOL/WEAK/AGGRO?

_____

SOLVING PROBLEMS THE RIGHT WAY

Robert wants to join a special gang at school. The leader of the gang tells him that if he goes to the newsagent and steals a pen and rubber, he can join the gang. Robert *really* wants to be accepted into the group.

STOP: What is the problem?

_____

_____

How does Robert feel?

_____

_____

THINK: What are three (3) things Robert could do, and what would be the likely result of each?

1. He could _____

_____

and the consequence might be _____

_____

2. He could _____

_____

and the consequence might be _____

_____

3. He could _____

_____

and the consequence might be _____

_____

DO: What do you think is the RIGHT thing to do?

_____

Is that COOL/WEAK/AGGRO? _____

SOLVING PROBLEMS THE RIGHT WAY

Ben is playing around with cigarettes and matches with you and some other friends behind the shed in the school yard. His teacher, Mr. Bates warned him before of the dangers involved with matches. Suddenly, you see Mr. Bates coming across the yard and yell out to the others to run. Mr. Bates catches Ben with the matches and cigarettes. He telephones Ben's mother and father to come to the school.

STOP: What is the problem?

_____

How does Ben feel? _____

_____

How do you feel? _____

_____

How does Mr. Bates feel? _____

_____

How do Ben's parents feel? _____

_____

THINK: What can Ben do?

1. _____

2. _____

3. _____

What can you do?

1. _____

2. _____

3. _____

What can Mr. Bates do?

1. _____

2. _____

3. _____

What can Ben's Parents do?

1. _____

2. _____

3. _____

DO: What do you think is the RIGHT thing for:-

Ben to do?_____

Is this COOL/WEAK/AGGRO?

You to do? _____

Is this COOL/WEAK/AGGRO?

Mr. Bates to do? _____

Is this COOL/WEAK/AGGRO?

Ben's parents to do? _____

Is this COOL/WEAK/AGGRO?

SOCIAL SKILLS TRAINING PROGRAMME FOR 7 — 12 YEAR OLDS
SESSION 8: GROUP PROBLEM SOLVING THE CO-OPERATIVE WAY

Aims of Session 8

- to discuss the notion that we all belong to groups; social, sporting, family, school.
- to illustrate that for groups to function, especially when making decisions or performing tasks for the benefit of the group, individual members need to co-operate with each other.
- to demonstrate that the CO-OPERATIVE way in group problem solving is often the FRIENDLY way and the COOL way (speaking up for yourself while considering and respecting others).
- to apply this concept to the planning of a farewell party.

Materials Required

- attendance chart, stickers, STOP-THINK-DO and COOL/WEAK/AGGRO posters, paper, textas.
- video recorder and monitor.
- video of "The Project" from "What Should I Do?" series or description /roleplay of similar social problem situation.
- materials suitable for play session which promote group planning and co-operation between members e.g. puppets and props for a puppet play production; dress-up clothes for a drama production; team games like "over and under", "tunnelball".
- homework for Session 8 is affixed during the session.

Procedure

1. Review last session and homework exercise.
   - the pressures of being a friend
   - is doing what you think is RIGHT always the FRIENDLY or COOL way? Check the homework for clues.
   - to decide what is the right thing to do, you need to evaluate the possible consequences, short and long term, of your decision.
2. Record points for attendance and homework completion on chart.
3. Group Problem Solving

   Ask the children to name the groups to which they belong — cubs, church group, basketball team etc. We all belong to a number of different groups — family, school, social, sporting. For a group to function properly, the individual people in the group cannot always have their own way or there would be continual conflict and the group would fall apart. Recall that in the first session of this Social Skills Group, we made rules which were fair to everyone. (Recap rules). If the children in the group had not co-operated with these rules and had just wanted their own way, the group would not have been able to work as it has. Co-operation is the key for groups to function properly.
4. Group Problem Solving Video "The Project"
   Some parents may participate at this point.

   This video portrays how the group process breaks down when the individual members are not co-operative. Divide into two groups to discuss using the STOP-THINK-DO method. Emphasize that when all members of a group co-operate, especially when there is work to be done or a function to perform, then all members are able to enjoy the result.

72

Behaving the CO-OPERATIVE way in a group is usually the COOL and FRIENDLY way — speaking up for yourself and giving your own ideas while being considerate of other people's ideas.

5. Group Problem Solving Applied

Planning a farewell party.

Elicit suggestions from the children regarding

-   what tasks need doing
-   what things are to be brought from home
-   what activities are to be arranged to make the party a success for all. Record on paper.
-   older children may elect a leader to co-ordinate planning.

Examples of tasks that need doing include:—

decorating room

making up drinks

setting up tables and chairs

setting out plates and cutlery

cutting cakes, fruit

cooking (if applicable)

cleaning up

Examples of items which need to be brought from home include:—

ingredients (e.g. for pancakes)

party food, drinks

music tapes

games

Examples of activities which need to be arranged:—

party games (e.g. pass the parcel)

timing of activities (e.g. eat or play first)

Encourage each child to make a commitment to co-operate in specific tasks and activities and to bring specific items from home. These are recorded in the homework books. It is advisable to mention the party and each child's commitment to the parents at the end of their session.

6. Play Session

Provide the opportunity for group activities which require consultation between members and co-operation in decision making e.g. team games, or drama/ puppet play production which may be performed for other group members or leaders.

7. Homework

Thinking about saying goodbye. Remembering the personal commitment to the farewell party.

Homework: Session 8 (for younger children)
GROUP PROBLEM SOLVING THE CO-OPERATIVE WAY

Next week is the last session and you will be saying goodbye to some of the friends you have met in this group.

STOP: What is the problem?

_____

_____

How do you feel?

_____

What do you want to happen? _____

_____

THINK: What can you do?

_____

1. _____

2. _____

3. _____

DO: What will you choose to do?

_____

_____

_____

REMEMBER   The farewell party is next week. If we all co-operate, we will all have fun.

What have you agreed to bring? _____

_____

What tasks and activities have you agreed to help with? _____

_____

Homework: Session 8 (for older children)
GROUP PROBLEM SOLVING THE CO-OPERATIVE WAY

1. Have you had any problems with someone in your family this week?

    What happened? _____

    _____

    How did you solve the problem? _____

    _____

2. Have you had any problems with someone in school this week? _____

    How did you solve the problem? _____

    _____

    What happened? _____

    _____

3. Next week is the last session and you will be saying goodbye to some of the friends you have met in this group.

STOP: What is the problem? _____

_____

How do you feel?

_____

What do you want to happen? _____

_____

THINK: What can you do?

_____

1. _____

2. _____

3. _____

DO: What will you choose to do?

_____

_____

REMEMBER   The farewell party is next week. If we all co-operate, we will all have fun.

What have you agreed to bring? _____

_____

What tasks and activities have you agreed to help with? _____

_____

SOCIAL SKILLS TRAINING PROGRAMME FOR 7 — 12 YEAR OLDS
SESSION 9: SAYING GOODBYE

Aims of Session 9

- to discuss the issue of saying goodbye.
- to utilize the farewell party as a co-operative group exercise.
- to evaluate goal achievement for the children.
- to determine the generalization of positive outcomes to school and home.

Materials Required

- attendance chart, STOP-THINK-DO and COOL/WEAK/AGGRO posters.
- goal sheets completed in earlier weeks fixed on wall. Include the children's comments from Session 1 on why they are coming to the group and what they hope to achieve; group goal sheets from Session 3 on what other children want them to do more often; goal sheets from Session 6 on how to be a better friend.
- for Pass the Parcel

    make up usual package for pass the parcel. On each layer of paper, have a message suitable for the age of the children in the group and relevant to the group programme e.g.

    "What do you do/say when you STOP?"

    "What do you do/say when you THINK (or DO)?"

    "What is a COOL way to solve a problem?"

    "What does a friend do/say?"

    "How does your imaginary shield help you solve problems?"

    "What goals have you achieved in the group?"

    "Describe one problem you solved using STOP-THINK-DO".
- audio tape player and music tapes for pass the parcel.
- furniture, equipment, decorations for party.
- Self Report Forms: POST GROUP (Appendix 13) and pens.
- rewards for children to choose.

Procedure

1. Review last session and homework exercise.
    - groups can only function when all members co-operate — then all feel okay.
    - relate this to planning of farewell party and see how we can co-operate as a group. Check that children have remembered their tasks and what to bring.
    - saying goodbye as a problem to solve. As solutions, encourage them to record telephone numbers, addresses in their homework books to enable them to keep in touch.
2. Record points for attendance and homework completion on chart.
3. Review Group Goals

    Check goal sheets for each child. Ask each:—

    "Have you achieved your goals in the group?"

"Has this helped you achieve goals at school and at home?"

Encourage feedback from children about each other's progress as well. Record the comments for discussion at the parents' feedback meeting next week, and with the teachers.

4. Self Report Forms: POST GROUP   completed by children.

5. Farewell Party

Allow children to take the responsibility for the actual running of the party e.g. when to eat, when to have activities, who will decorate if these decisions have not already been made. The leader may suggest Pass the Parcel since this provides a final rehearsal of the concepts taught in the group programme. When the music stops, the child with the parcel unwraps it and must answer the question before passing it on, until eventually the surprise is unwrapped. The child may then decide whether it is shared.

Clearing up is also a group responsibility requiring co-operation.

6. Rewards

Choice of rewards for attendance and homework completion.

7. Goodbyes

Remind children of review session in 3 months.

8. Post Group Teacher Involvement

Following this session, group leaders initiate post group contact with the teachers involved in the programme.

School peer acceptance of the children in the group is evaluated following training intervention (see Chapter 6).

SOCIAL SKILLS TRAINING PROGRAMME FOR 7 — 12 YEAR OLDS
POST GROUP: EVALUATION

Aims

- to collate information received from teachers, parents, children and group leaders regarding the progress of children over the term of the group.

- to plan the feedback to parents in the following week.
- to discuss recommendations for further follow-up.

Materials Required

- completed forms (PRE GROUP) and (POST GROUP) from parents, teachers and children (self)
- goal achievement sheets completed in session 9 of the child group.
- completed Peer Rating Forms (PRE) and (POST)
- Social Skills Programme Evaluation Forms (Appendix 15).

Procedure

1. Following session 9 and the completion of the teacher forms, leaders of the child and parent groups meet to evaluate progress and goal achievement for the children and parents in the training programme.

2. Rating Scales Evaluation

   a) Compare the ratings from the PRE and POST group assessments obtained from parents, teachers and children on the various scales reflecting social competence and social skills deficits. Specifically, a comparison of the PRE and POST group ratings will reflect trends or changes in
      - peer acceptance
      - attention seeking behaviour
      - aggressiveness (physical & verbal)
      - self-confidence
      - ability to cope with teasing
      - maturity
      - ability to make and keep friends.

   b) Compare also the relative strengths and weaknesses of these trends from the various significant viewpoints monitored during the term of the training programme (parents, teachers, children, group leaders).

   c) Assess change in peer ratings of social acceptability and likability for target children compared with "control" children included in the assessment. Compare also changes in peer ratings with trends identified by teachers, parents, group leaders, and the children themselves in terms of improved social acceptability. Evaluate positive trends for other than the target children in terms of the estimated effectiveness of the teacher training programme and the competence of the teachers in implementing classroom social skills programmes.

3. Goal Achievement

   Assess goal achievement from the various viewpoints. Include an assessment of the goals achieved by the parents attending the parent group.

4. Recommendations

   Suggestions for further management may include

   — follow-up involvement in social skills training programme for "booster" sessions.

   — referral to local resources or community groups e.g. cubs, youth organizations, community health clinic, Education Department resource (or equivalent in private school system).

   — referral for specialist input if specific problems have been identified in the group e.g. specific learning difficulty, co-ordination problems, hearing difficulties, possible organic dysfunction, marital problems, sexual abuse.

5. Prepare summaries for feedback to parents in session 10. (Refer to Parent Training Programme, session 10).

6. Written Reports

   Following session 10, the leaders of the children's group complete Social Skills Programme Evaluation Reports on the children for whom they are responsible in the group. These reports are made available to parents, teachers and the referring persons.

SOCIAL SKILLS TRAINING PROGRAMME FOR 7 — 12 YEAR OLDS
REVIEW: MAINTENANCE AND GENERALIZATION

Aims of Review

- to renew acquaintances.
- to evaluate goal maintenance over three month period.
- to evaluate generalization of positive outcomes over school and home environments and different social situations.
- to make further recommendations for management and goal attainment.

Materials Required

- large sheets of paper, textas, toys, STOP-THINK-DO and COOL/WEAK/AGGRO posters
- goal sheets completed during the group sessions fixed on the wall
- Self Report Forms: REVIEW (Appendix 14) and pens

Procedure

1. Renew acquaintances

   Discuss contacts maintained between the children in the group. Discuss feelings about this meeting compared with the first group session.

2. Maintenance of Goals

   Refer each child to the goals set and achieved during the term of the group. Check whether they have maintained the goals they achieved. Record their responses. Discuss what they might do to re-establish their goals if they have not been maintained. Use a STOP-THINK-DO approach to this problem and encourage all children to participate in the discussions. Additionally, check if children have new goals which they would like to achieve. Use STOP-THINK-DO to discuss how they might achieve these goals.

3. Self Report Forms: REVIEW completed by children.

4. Play Session (about ½ hour)

   While play is progressing, one leader monitors using STOP-THINK-DO while the other leader joins parent group to discuss the children for whom they have taken responsibility. They exchange roles half-way through playtime.

5. Parent Feedback

   A leader from child group joins the parent group to

   — discuss the children's progress in social areas particularly related to the home and the maintenance of goals achieved in the group. Check over the information provided by the children and parents in their REVIEW forms.

   — discuss the teachers' comments regarding progress and their ratings of the children on the REVIEW forms.

   — make recommendations for future management.

   — discuss school peer acceptance of each child from peer ratings.

6. Final Note

   A brief report on progress is made to the persons who initially referred the children to the Social Skills training programme.

Chapter 4
Social Skills
Training Programme
for Young Adolescents

Chapter 4:
Social Skills Training Programme
For Young Adolescents

OUTLINE

SOCIAL SKILLS TRAINING PROGRAMME FOR YOUNG ADOLESCENTS
SESSION 1:GETTING TO KNOW YOU

Aims of Session 1

- to learn how to meet new people.
- to identify each young person's social motivation in terms of their goals for group attendance.
- to get to know more about each other, the similarities and differences by looking carefully and listening to each other.
- to encourage group identity and trust between members.
- to establish rules for behaviour in the group.
- to outline group programme.
- to encourage regular attendance.

Materials Required

- comfortable chairs placed in a circle.
- individual tags with name of each young person and leader to be used in first few weeks.
- Self Report Forms: PRE GROUP (Appendix 12) and pens.
- group rules displayed on poster.
- attendance chart with name of each person and 9 columns for recording attendance and homework completion each week.
- exercise book for each person to be used as a diary for regular recording of problem situations and progress. Formal homework for session 1 is affixed during the session.
- large sheets of paper.
- textas.
- refreshments.

Procedure

1. Young people are welcomed to group and asked to take a seat.
2. Self Report Forms: PRE GROUP completed by adolescents.

   Explain and discuss each question, particularly the reference to goal identification.
3. Meeting People

   Name tags are placed face down in the centre of a circle. A leader has name tag on, introduces self pleasantly while looking closely at each group member.

   Leader then chooses one tag and finds out to whom it belongs by questioning the children. When the person is identified by name, find out more about him/her by asking questions for example, about age, school, hobbies, sports, favourite TV programmes. The identified person then selects another name tag and repeats the above procedure with encouragement from leaders if necessary.
4. While introductions are proceeding, introduce the concepts of "same — different" by recognizing the similarities and differences in the people present. Emphasize that it is okay for people to be different and like different things — it makes meeting people interesting.

5. Following the introductions, discuss rules for meeting people for the first time:—
   — Approach them face to face
   — look at their eyes
   — smile and say hello
   — tell them your name
   — ask them questions about themselves
   — listen to them

6. Feeling Recognition and Expression

   By looking at others carefully, and by listening to them we can get to know them better. We can pick up their feelings about certain things more accurately. Encourage the children to describe the cues they use to detect people's feelings. How can we tell? The most reliable cues are facial expressions, body gestures, voice tone and quality.

7. Personal Goals

   Ask children why they are attending the group and what they would like to achieve. Leaders may refer to their comments on the Self Report forms just completed. Discuss the similarities and differences in their reasons and goals. Pay close attention to any feelings expressed by the children in this discussion. Record answers on paper for future reference.

8. Break (10 minutes)

   A short break for refreshments offers an opportunity for informal conversation and relaxation.

9. Group Rules

   Discuss why we need rules in a group — so that everyone has a fair go. Rules (on poster) may include
   — only one person speaks at a time while others listen
   — everyone has a chance to speak if they want to
   — if anyone gets too excited, rough, noisy or otherwise distracts the group, they will be asked to settle down.
   Discuss penalties for breaking rules since the whole group suffers from disruptive behaviour which prevents effective group functioning. Encourage all members to contribute ideas about penalties and to take on the responsibility of reminding each other about the rules and penalties if necessary.

10. Programme Outline

    Suggest the following outline

    Weeks 2,3,4 — adolescents will be taught to LOOK & LISTEN to find out more about others, including their feelings, and to STOP & THINK before rushing into anything when interpersonal problems arise.

    Week 5 — free session to be planned by group members.

    Weeks 6,7,8 — after STOP & THINK comes DO. Evaluating our social behaviour according to a number of different criteria.

    Week 9 — free session, farewell party.

11. Parent & Teacher Involvement

    Discuss the nature of the concurrent parent programme. Parents will aim to model and reinforce their children's newly learned skills in the home related environment. Discuss the participation of teachers in the programme with the aim to generalize skills to the school situation. Elicit feelings of group members about this involvement.

12. Encourage Regular Commitment

Explain the need for regular weekly attendance and the completion of homework. 1 point is earned for regular diary entries and/or set homework per week, which are recorded on the attendance chart. Record points for session 1 attendance. People must earn 6 points to participate in week 5 activities, and 12 points for week 9 activities. Encourage also daily diary entries about particular problems and solutions utilized.

13. Formal Homework

Children record their thoughts and feelings about their attendance at the Social Skills group. Encourage the use of diaries to record events and problem situations for discussion in the next session, if they wish.

14. Collect name tags before saying goodbye.

15. Pre Group Teacher Involvement

Following the session, group leaders initiate the first contact (termed — PRE GROUP) with the teachers of the adolescents whose parents have given permission (see Chapter 6).

Homework: Session 1

GETTING TO KNOW YOU

You have just finished your first session in the Social Skills group.

How do you feel?

_____

What goals do you hope to achieve by attending the group? _____

_____

_____

How can the people in this group help you achieve your goals? _____

_____

_____

How can the parent who is attending the parent group help you achieve your goals? _____

_____

_____

How can your teacher help you achieve your goals? _____

_____

_____

Write down a suggestion for an activity we can do in the group which will help us get to know each

other better? _____

_____

_____

SOCIAL SKILLS TRAINING PROGRAMME FOR YOUNG ADOLESCENTS
SESSION 2: RECOGNIZING AND EXPRESSING FEELINGS

Aims of Session 2

- to demonstrate feeling expression through body gestures, facial expressions and voice tones.
- to establish plans of action for goal achievement for each adolescent through personal feedback and reinforcement within the supportive group.
- to identify the role of parents and teachers in goal attainment.
- to further encourage group identity and trust.

Materials Required

- name tags, group rules poster, attendance chart, textas, large sheets of paper (as per last session)
- note paper and pens
- for Blindfold Encounter
  - large handkerchiefs for use as blindfolds
  - obstacles eg. boxes, chairs, string across the room above ground level
- homework for Session 2 to be affixed during the session.
- refreshments.

Procedure

1. Name tags are placed face down on the floor in centre of the circle of chairs. Each person picks up one tag and tries to locate its owner by memory or asking around, and then pins on the tag.

2. Review last session.
   - rules for meeting people
   - group rules
   - getting to know about someone by looking carefully at them and asking questions
   - how did people feel after last session?

3. Record points for attendance and homework completion on chart.

4. Getting to Know More about You

   The aim of this activity is to get to know a little more about each other and build group cohesiveness. Each person takes a piece of paper and pen, all stand and form pairs. Each pair finds **one** thing the partners have in common — e.g. a favourite T.V. programme or musical group, the most hated subject at school, only one parent at home. When a common thing has been found, each writes it down next to their partner's name. Each pair has only **2 minutes** for discussion. Leaders call time and the pairs break up. Each person immediately forms a pair with someone else and is given 2 minutes to find something in common which they both write down as above. This exercise is repeated until everyone has remet. The group then reforms and discusses the new information. Encourage the expression of feelings about the commonalities found between members e.g. by saying "I can see by the look on your face that *(the common dislike)* really annoys you." *(Describe the drawn mouth and frowning forehead).* "I can also tell by the tone of your voice". *(Check with the look and sound when they describe it).*

5. Personal Goals (from homework exercise)

Divide into two small groups, each with a leader, to discuss the following homework questions:—

How can the people in this group help you achieve your goals?

Discuss the various suggestions which may include:—

by teaching me new ways of handling social situations and relationships

by giving me feedback about how I appear to others

by letting me talk out my worries rather than act them out

by not putting me down for my problems.

How can the parent who is attending the parent group help you achieve your goals?

Suggestions may include:—

by helping me practice new skills at home

by not putting me down for my problem

by explaining to others in my family what we are learning in the group

by letting me talk out my worries at home.

How can your teacher help you achieve your goals?

Suggestions may include:—

by helping me practice new skills at school

by not putting me down for my problems

by encouraging me to talk about my worries at school to the teacher or school counsellor

by explaining to other teachers (and maybe, students) what I am learning in the group, and encouraging their support.

6. Break (10 minutes)

Refreshments and conversation.

7. Blindfold Encounter

Young people form pairs. One of each pair is blindfolded. Pairs stand together at one end of room. Obstacles are placed over the floor and across the room. Children must physically lead their blindfolded mates safely across the room without saying anything. Each pair then exchanges the blindfold. This time, children must guide their blindfolded partners through the obstacle course to the other side of the room using only verbal instructions and cues but no physical contact. The aim of the encounter is to promote trust and co-operation, as well as to emphasize the importance of careful looking and listening skills.

8. Personal Feedback

Form a group. Ask members individually to give one word to describe a particular person in the group. Check with the person whether the descriptions match his/her self-perceptions. Repeat for all team members. Discuss the implications of such feedback and its influence on self-concept.

9. Suggested Activities

Refer to last week's homework and suggested activities for the group. Discuss the various ideas and allow time this session or next to try out the more popular activities.

10.   Diary Entries

Ask for volunteers to share diary entries with the rest of the group. If problem situations have been recorded ask the following:—

What happened?

How did you feel?

How did the other person(s) feel?

How could you tell how they felt?

What did you do to solve the problem?

Did it work?

What else could you have done?

Brainstorm solutions.

11.   Homework

An exercise on getting to know about feelings.

12.   Leaders' Meeting

Leaders from both adolescent and parent groups meet for a discussion re:

—   the adolescents' views of their social problems and goals for themselves.

—   the parents' views of their childrens' problems and goals for children and selves.

—   the teachers' views of the childrens' problems and goals for the children attending the group.

—   the group leaders' analyses of the adolescents from observations in the group sessions.

On the basis of this discussion, goals are determined for each adolescent and parent which will be reinforced in the remaining group sessions.

Homework: Session 2
RECOGNIZING AND EXPRESSING FEELING

1. **What is something you do or say which makes your mother feel sad?**

   _____

   _____

   How can you tell she feels sad?

   Draw how she looks:

   Write down how she sounds _____

   _____

2. **What is something you do or say which makes your brother/sister happy?**

   _____

   _____

   How can you tell he/she feels happy?

   Draw how he/she looks:

   Write down how he/she sounds _____

   _____

3. **What is something you do or say which makes your friend at school angry?** _____

   How can you tell your friend feels angry? _____

   Draw how he/she looks:

   Write down how he/she sounds _____

   _____

4. **What is something your friend does or says to you which makes you feel embarrassed?**

_____

_____

How do you look and sound when you feel embarrassed?

_____

_____

5. **What is something your father does or says to you which makes you feel scared?**

_____

_____

How do you look and sound when you feel scared

_____

_____

6. **What is something that someone in this group did or said to you which made you feel good about yourself?**

_____

_____

Don't forget to use your diary this week

SOCIAL SKILLS TRAINING GROUP FOR YOUNG ADOLESCENTS
SESSION 3: SOLVING SOCIAL PROBLEMS WITH STOP-THINK-DO

Aims of Session 3

- to reinforce prosocial behaviour through positive feedback within the supportive group.
- to encourage the appreciation of causes or reasons for feelings.
  "Why does she feel like that? Because.....happened".
- to emphasize that feelings also cause us to behave in certain ways, often without thinking.
- to teach the STOP-THINK-DO step by step approach to social problems using the traffic light motto.

STOP (red)	—	define problems
	—	recognize feelings
	—	identify goals
THINK (yellow)	—	generate solutions
	—	evaluate consequences
DO (green)	—	choose solution
	—	initiate action

- to prepare adolescents for teachers' feedback following the session

Materials Required

- group rules poster, attendance chart, textas, large sheets of paper
- STOP-THINK-DO posters (Appendix 18)
- video recorder and monitor
- video of "The New Girl" from the "What Should I Do?" series (Additional Resource Materials). If video is unavailable a social problem situation may be described or roleplayed (see homework exercises).
- homework for session 3 to be affixed during the session.

Procedure

1. Review last session.
   - getting to know more about ourselves and each other
   - what things we have in common
   - how we appear to others
   - whether we can trust each other and co-operate as a group
   - a group activity suggested by someone last week might be inserted at this point.

2. Record points for attendance and homework on chart.

3. Feelings and Their Causes (from homework exercises)
   Charades
   Form pairs. Each person chooses a situation described for homework and enlists the aid

of a partner to devise a charade about the feeling and what caused it. Thus, each pair, in turn, will roleplay two feeling situations without words, using only actions, body gestures and facial expressions. The rest of the group has to guess the situation and the feeling. Discuss the notion that while feelings have causes, they also cause us to behave in certain ways, often without thinking whether it is a good idea or not.

4. Personal Feedback

Discuss the answers to the homework question about what someone in the group did or said to make someone else feel good about him/herself. Encourage each person to direct comments to the person concerned e.g. while looking at Brian, Judy says "I felt good when Brian said he liked my idea for an activity last week". Leader reflects back to the person speaking their apparent positive feelings by the look on their face, use of eye-contact, tone of voice.

5. Break (10 minutes)

Refreshments and conversation.

6. STOP-THINK-DO

Discuss the concept already raised about how feelings cause us to behave in certain ways, often without thinking whether it is a good idea or not. Show the video of "The New Girl". Although it is a cartoon, young adolescents still seem to appreciate this format. It is relevant to the issue of meeting people and joining into groups. It also serves to introduce the STOP-THINK-DO approach to social problem solving, and the traffic light motto:—

STOP (red)   *"Look at the problem before you rush into anything."*

"Don't get carried away by your feelings."   .

"What is happening?"

"How did she/would you feel?"

"What would you want to happen if you were her?"

Discuss the goals the group members would have if they were in the same situation.

THINK (yellow)   *"What could she/would you do to solve the problem?"*

"What would happen if she/you did that.... or that.....or that?"

"How would you/she feel then?"

DO (green)   *"Pick the solution with the most acceptable consequences and do it!"*

"If it doesn't work, try another solution. There is always an answer if you stop and think about it."

7. Problem Solving Applied

Divide into 2 groups, each with a leader. Ask for volunteers to discuss problem situations recorded in their diaries during the week. Apply the STOP-THINK-DO approach to each problem. Elicit as many different solutions as possible from group members. Evaluate each in terms of possible consequences. Obtain opinions on the best solution. Encourage the people who owned the problems to write them down and give them a try if the problems arise again. Urge them to record the results in their diaries for future reference.

8. Preparation for Teacher Training Session.

   Advise the group of the teachers' meeting following this session. Record the responses of each person to the questions:—

   "What do you think your teacher will say about you?"

   "What would he/she want you to achieve by attending the group?"

   These comments are useful to discuss with the teachers.

9. Homework

   Applying the STOP-THINK-DO approach to a personal problem.

SOLVING SOCIAL PROBLEMS WITH STOP-THINK-DO

A problem I had this week

What happened. _____

_____

_____

_____

How I felt. _____

_____

_____

How others felt. _____

_____

_____

What I wanted to happen. _____

_____

_____

What I did to solve the problem. _____

_____

_____

What happened next. _____

_____

_____

What else I could have done. _____

_____

_____

What would have been the best thing to do. _____

_____

_____

SOCIAL SKILLS TRAINING PROGRAMME FOR YOUNG ADOLESCENTS
SESSION 4: SOLVING PROBLEMS THE COOL WAY

Aims of Session 4

- to teach adolescents to differentiate Cool, Weak and Aggro response styles

  COOL ———— politely assertive

  WEAK ———— passive

  AGGRO ———— aggressive

- to encourage adolescents to categorize solutions generated in the THINK step of the STOP-THINK-DO method according to the COOL/WEAK/AGGRO criteria.

- to emphasize that the COOL way of behaving often leads to the most acceptable consequences and is therefore useful to try first to solve social problems.

- to discuss teacher feedback in terms of the identification and compatibility of goals from teachers' and adolescents' perspectives.

- to encourage group co-operation through planning of outing for following session.

Materials Required

- group rules poster, attendance chart, textas, paper, STOP-THINK-DO, COOL/WEAK/AGGRO posters (Appendix 19).

- video camera and monitor.

- sheets from last session recording expectations re teachers' comments and goals

- homework for session 4 to be affixed during the session

Procedure

1. Review last session.
   - feelings have causes (Why do you feel...? Because....happened)
   - feelings also cause us to behave in certain ways, often without thinking
   - STOP-THINK-DO approach (recall traffic light motto) gives us alternative ways of handling our feelings and solving our problems.

2. Record attendance and homework completion on chart.

3. Solving Social Problems with Cool Assertiveness

   This section may be video taped and replayed for closer observation. Select a problem situation from the homework exercises which could be solved by politely assertive behaviour e.g. a person wants to join in an activity in which others are already involved. They virtually ignore the person when he/she asks to be included. Roleplay the situation with one leader taking the role of the person trying to join in.

   Refer to poster for verbal, non-verbal and emotional characteristics of the cool, weak and aggro response styles.

   AGGRO

   The leader first roleplays an aggressive solution e.g. pushes way into group and makes demands. The other leader calls "STOP" and asks the group to discuss the technique used in terms of facial expression, body gesture, voice tone, feelings conveyed.

A person who is behaving in an AGGRO way:—

shouts, yells

speaks rudely, abuses, teases, puts down

blames others

looks mad

stands close and threatens

pushes, hits, kicks

feels angry, annoyed, out of control

Discuss also the possible consequence of such behaviour."What could happen next?" Contrive the roleplay showing a number of possible consequences or results of such aggro behaviour. Finally, evaluate the effectiveness of this method for solving the person's problem of wanting to join in the activity.

WEAK

The leader then roleplays a very passive response, e.g. stands to the side of the group and sulks. The other leader calls "STOP" and discusses the technique used in terms of facial expression, body gesture, voice tone, feelings conveyed.

A person who is behaving in a WEAK WAY:—

talks softly, mumbles

cries or sulks when faced with a problem

looks down at the floor

stands far away, hunched over

gives in to others

feels shy, embarrassed, nervous, useless, unhappy

Look at the possible consequences of such behaviour. "What could happen next?" Continue the roleplay showing a number of possible results of such weak behaviour.

Evaluate the effectiveness of this method for solving the person's problem.

COOL

The leader then roleplays a reasonably assertive response e.g. approaching someone and asking firmly and positively. Other leader again leads the discussion about the technique used in terms of facial expression, body gesture, voice tone, feelings conveyed.

A person who is behaving in a COOL way (like Fonzie in "Happy Days"):—

speaks firmly but friendly

stands up for self politely

smiles or looks calm

stands tall

looks other person in the eyes

feels happy, confident, in control, okay about self

Discuss the possible consequences of such COOL behaviour. Roleplay these and evaluate the effectiveness of this method of problem solving. Encourage the child who originally described the problem for homework to evaluate the technique they used in terms of COOL/WEAK/AGGRO and the consequences of their action.

4. Evaluating Consequences

Break into two groups, each with a leader. Evaluate the other problems and solutions described in the homework exercise according to whether the response was politely assertive (COOL), passive (WEAK) or aggressive (AGGRO). Compare the consequences of COOL, WEAK and AGGRO responses and how the person feels afterwards.

Emphasize that the COOL way generally has the most acceptable consequences, and is therefore often the solution to choose and try first.

5. Break (10 minutes)

Refreshments and conversation

6. Feedback from Teacher Training Session

Match the adolescents' predictions about what their teachers would say about them with the actual comments made at the teacher session. Discuss discrepancies and commonalities. Check also the goals which the teachers would like the children to achieve from the teachers' comments and rating form responses.

Pose the questions:—

"Do you want to achieve these goals?"

If yes,

"How can the members of this group help you achieve these goals?"

Obtain a commitment from the members to 'be helpful'.

7. Group Co-operation

Check the attendance chart to discern who is eligible for participation in the week 5 outing. If all children are not eligible, consider this as a problem situation to be worked through in the STOP-THINK-DO way to reach a solution with consequences which are acceptable to all. Further decisions which require attention include — the nature and location of the outing, meeting place, the cost, transport, time restrictions, inclusion of parents. The final decisions need to be made by group consensus and then fed back to the parent group.

Suitable suggestions include ice/roller skating or other sporting activities, amusement parks/arcades. Such establishments are often willing to provide concessions.

8. Homework

A COOL/WEAK/AGGRO analysis of solutions to interpersonal problems.

SOLVING PROBLEMS THE COOL WAY

Joanne is in your class at school. She hasn't been at your school very long and doesn't seem to have made many friends. Everyone calls her a "nerd" because she is very serious and only seems interested in studying. Lately, she seems to look for you to sit next to in Science lessons but you don't want the others to shun you like they do her.

1. STOP: What is the problem?

_____

_____

How does Joanne feel?

_____

How do you feel? _____

_____

2. THINK: What can Joanne do to solve the problem? and
What would be the likely result?

_____

1. She could _____

    and the consequence might be _____

_____

2. She could _____

    and the consequence might be _____

_____

3. She could _____

    and the consequence might be _____

_____

What can you do and what would be the result?

1. I could _____

    and the consequence might be _____

_____

2. I could _____

  and the consequence might be _____

_____

3. I could _____

  and the consequence might be _____

_____

3. DO: What is the best thing for Joanne to do?

_____

Is this COOL/ WEAK/ AGGRO? _____

What is the best thing for you to do? _____

_____

Is this COOL/ WEAK/ AGGRO? _____

_____

4.   Do you ever get teased or put down? _____

How are you teased or put down? _____

_____

What do you do? _____

_____

What would be a COOL thing to do? _____

_____

We will talk more about teasing after our group outing next week.

5.   What things do you need to remember for our outing next week? _____

_____

_____

SOCIAL SKILLS TRAINING PROGRAMME FOR YOUNG ADOLESCENTS
SESSION 5: REAL LIFE PRACTICE WITHIN A SUPPORTIVE GROUP

Aims of Session

- to promote group identity and cohesion.
- to enhance generalization of newly learned social problem solving skills to a more natural peer related environment.
- to identify social skills or skills deficits which may not be evident in the more structured group setting.
- to have fun.

Procedure

1. Children, parents and leaders meet for a shared lunch.
2. Parent group may then follow on as usual while children leave for their group outing, following the plans made last session.
3. Photographs taken during the outing provide both enjoyment and a reference for future session.
4. Several issues may be raised and discussed as the outing proceeds.
   - looking and listening carefully to each other
   - recognizing and expressing feelings
   - thinking before acting
   - evaluating behaviour as COOL/WEAK/AGGRO
   - evaluating consequences of behaviour
   - handling unfriendly behaviour (teasing, cheating)
   - individual differences in likes, habits, feelings, behaviour
   - group rules versus individual goals
   - fairness and co-operation
   - appropriate/inappropriate behaviour and the attention it receives
   - handling authority inside and outside the group
   - the "right" way to behave
   - the leadership role
   - relating this group experience to other groups the young people belong to (school, family, sport, social)
   - goals in particular social situations
5. Return from outing as a group.
6. Homework

   Record feelings, comments about the outing for discussion next week.
7. Leaders' Meeting

   Following the session, leaders from parent and adolescent groups meet to review progress and evaluate goals for children and parents.

Homework: Session 5
REAL LIFE PRACTICE WITHIN A SUPPORTIVE GROUP

1. What things did you like about the group outing? _____

    _____

2. What things didn't you like? _____

    _____

3. Describe a problem you had with someone else.

    What happened? _____

    _____

    How did you feel? _____

    How did the other person feel? _____

    What did you do to solve the problem? _____

    Is this COOL/WEAK/AGGRO? _____

    What happened after that? _____

    How did you feel then? _____

    How did the other person feel? _____

    Is there a better way you could have handled the problem? _____

    _____

    Is this COOL/WEAK/AGGRO? _____

4. Did someone do or say a friendly thing to you on the outing?

    Who did/said it? _____

    What did they do/say? _____

    How did you feel? _____

SOCIAL SKILLS TRAINING PROGRAMME FOR YOUNG ADOLESCENTS
SESSION 6: SOLVING PROBLEMS THE FRIENDLY WAY

Aims of Session 6
- to build on the group cohesiveness provided by the outing.
- to increase motivation for behaving in a friendly way by identifying and reinforcing prosocial goals for each child in the supportive group environment.
- to emphasize that to have friends you have to behave like one.
- to teach children to recognize friendly ways of behaving when solving social problems. FRIENDLY — fair, co-operative, considerate and respectful of others.
- to demonstrate that the FRIENDLY way of behaving is generally compatible with the COOL way.
- to instruct children in effective ways of handling unfriendly behaviour, especially teasing and put downs.

Materials Required
- attendance chart, STOP-THINK-DO and COOL/WEAK/AGGRO posters, large sheets of paper, textas
- friendliness sheets

  on individual sheets of paper, write each child's name and a line down the centre of the page. On one half of the page write "What does....do or say that is friendly? On the other half write "How could ... be a better friend?"
- refreshments
- homework for session 6 to be affixed during the session

Procedure
1. Informal Discussion re Group Outing

   Refer to homework question 1 & 2 for comments and criticisms regarding the outing. Allow informal discussion to recap enjoyable times and promote group cohesiveness and identity. Make refreshments available at this stage to add to relaxed atmosphere.
2. Record points for attendance and homework completion on chart.
3. Problem Solving Applied: Personal Feedback

   To discuss question 3 of the homework, ask each person to pair up with the person with whom they had the problem. Each pair may not have identified the same problem, so one discusses their situation first and then the other moves on to form a pair with the person with whom they had a problem and so on.... Encourage each pair to discuss the answers recorded and to match them with the other person's perceptions of the problem, their feelings and their solutions. Urge each pair to reach a consensus on what would have been the best way to handle the situation so that they both felt okay.

   It is to be expected that some children will be involved in more social problem situations than others and may therefore have to pair up with a number of people for this exercise, while others may not be involved at all. It is important to draw attention to such imbalances since these are probably a valid reflection of social functioning in real life. It also serves to make each person aware of the sorts of conflict situations in which they are likely to be involved, the types of solutions they are most likely to choose and also the effectiveness of these choices of action. When people are not involved directly in a pair, encourage them to act as a third person to an ongoing pair discussion. They may be able to offer alternative solutions and also reflect back the feelings of those involved more accurately. Leaders may take on this role for various pairs. When evaluating solutions, have them describe each solution in terms of COOL/WEAK/AGGRO criteria.

4. Friendship Discussion

    Return to large group

    Introduce the notion that to have or make a friend, you have to behave like one. Pose the questions:-

    "What is a friend?" Emphasize qualities like co-operation, consideration of others, fairness, respect, trust, loyalty, kindness as components of friendship. Do unto others...

    "What do you like about your friends?"

    "What do you do with your friends?"

    Let's look at these questions in terms of the friendships within the group.

5. Friendliness Sheets: Personal Feedback

    Place friendliness sheets (as prepared) separately on the wall or floor for this exercise. Refer to question 4 of the homework, and have members identify the people who did or said something friendly to them on the outing, find their sheet and record what they did or said. Then, encourage the children to record something for other members of the group who have done or said friendly things at any time. After this list is completed, have the children contemplate the other side of the page (How could .... be a better friend?) and record any suggestions they may have for each child. When finished, discuss as a group each person's friendliness sheet. Ask for ideas from the group members on how they can help each other become better friends. Leave the sheets on display to refer to during the session. Actively reinforce friendly behaviour throughout.

6. Handling Unfriendly Behaviour

    Discuss examples of people behaving in an unfriendly way towards each other, such as:—

    > pushing in front of others
    >
    > refusing to let them join in an activity
    >
    > being physically rough
    >
    > cheating in games
    >
    > teasing or put downs

    Refer back to homework from Week 4 about the girl who was put down for being a 'nerd' and new to the school. Check through the exercise and discuss the solutions suggested and the possible consequences of each. Look for a consensus regarding the best thing to do to handle negative behaviour from others from both Joanne's point of view and the other person's. Emphasize suggestions which are both COOL (i.e. appropriately assertive and confident) and FRIENDLY (i.e. fair and considerate of others) since these solutions are more likely to have consequences which are acceptable to more people.

    Ask the children to recall times when they were teased or put down, how they felt and how they reacted. Following the above discussion, do they now have any better ways of handling such teasing, stirring or put downs?

    Some younger adolescents find useful the erection of an imaginary shield around them which prevents unfriendly words/actions from reaching them. If considered appropriate for the group, discuss the concept, emphasizing that while they are THINKING about the shield (its colour or texture, the sound the words make bouncing off), they are not getting hurt or feeling bad about what is said to them. They then have more time to THINK of an appropriate way to handle the situation rather than just reacting in their usual but often ineffective way.

7. Homework

An exercise on friendly versus unfriendly behaviour, and how to handle the latter.

SOLVING PROBLEMS THE FRIENDLY WAY

1. **Choose one member of your family or a friend at school and write down the friendly and unfriendly things you say or do to that person, and that they say or do to you, during the week. How did these make you feel?**

Friendly things I said & did to	How I felt
1.	
2.	
3.	

Unfriendly things I said or did to	How I felt
1.	
2.	
3.	

Friendly things .... said or did to me	How I felt
1.	
2.	
3.	

Unfriendly things .... said or did to me	How I felt
1.	
2.	
3.	

2. **What is the best way for you to handle teasing or put downs from:**

    people your own age? _____

    parents? _____

    teachers? _____

3. **Has your imaginary shield helped you?** _____

    When? _____

SOCIAL SKILLS TRAINING PROGRAMME FOR YOUNG ADOLESCENTS
SESSION 7: SOLVING PROBLEMS THE RIGHT WAY

Aims of Session 7

- (building on last session) to discuss how to handle put downs (negative statements) from/to parents and teachers.
- to demonstrate the pressures of friendship on our choices of solutions to social problems involving moral issues.
- to illustrate that, in some situations, we may not feel that the FRIENDLY WAY (the way our friends would like us to behave) is the RIGHT way (the way our parents/others have taught us) or even the COOL way (standing up politely for ourselves).

  RIGHT — responsible, moral, expected.

- to emphasize that such conflicts can be resolved through an evaluation of short and long term consequences of each course of action in each particular situation.

Materials Required

- attendance chart, STOP-THINK-DO and COOL/WEAK/AGGRO posters, large sheets of paper
- friendliness sheets from last session fixed on the wall
- homework for session 7 affixed during session.

Procedure

1. Review last session.
   - how friends behave (refer to friendliness sheets)
   - the FRIENDLY way to solve problems is with fairness, co-operation, consideration and respect for others.
   - how to handle unfriendly behaviour, especially teasing and put downs.

2. Record points for attendance and homework completion.

3. Popular Parent Put downs

   Break into 2 smaller groups, each with a leader. Refer to homework exercise. Discuss the feelings which put downs and teasing arouse and how they are handled by the children. Note how their methods of coping vary, depending on who is involved — parent, teacher, peer, sibling. On a large sheet of paper, write "Popular Parent Put downs". Draw a line down the centre. On one side, list the children's nominations of the most commonly used negative statements to them by their parents. On the other side, list the children's choices of the most commonly used negative statements by them to their parents.

   Examples of put downs by parents

   "You're useless"

   "If you did some work occassionally,..."

   "We can't even talk to you anymore"

   "You're far too young to..."

   "Why don't you grow up?"

   "Why aren't you like your brother?"

   "Why don't you get some decent friends?"

   "How many times do I have to tell you?"

"No wonder you haven't got any friends".

"I haven't got time now".

Examples of put downs to parents

"Why aren't you like normal parents?"

"Don't you care?"

"You don't give a damn about me, anyway".

"Why won't you listen?"

"You never understand".

"Why don't you just leave me alone?"

"Don't you trust me?"

"It's your fault!"

"You're always too busy".

Have the adolescents think about the feelings aroused by these statements and the usual reactions they cause. Are there better ways of handling such unfriendly statements? Discuss alternative solutions in terms of COOL/WEAK/AGGRO, and also the likely consequences. How would everyone feel then?

4. Teacher Teasers

On sheets of paper write "Teacher Teasers". Draw a line down the centre. Repeat the above exercise using the most commonly used negative statements by/to teachers, by/to adolescents.

Relevant examples may be offered arising from the Teacher Training Sessions.

Examples of put downs by teachers

"You can't be trusted now".

"That was okay, BUT..."

"If you paid some attention in class,..."

"Of course, I would expect that from you".

"I've explained it 100 times!"

"I don't believe you".

"Why do you bother coming to school?"

"You're old enough to handle your own problems".

"What will your parents think of you?"

Examples of put downs to teachers

"Don't you trust me?"

"History was much better with Mr. Lawrence".

"You didn't tell us we have homework".

"I thought you were supposed to teach us".

"It's no point coming to you, you won't do anything about it".

Discuss the feelings aroused and usual reactions such statements cause. Evaluate alternative ways of handling such statements and likely consequences.

5. Break (10 minutes)

Refreshments and conversation. Children may like to informally discuss diary entries with each other or leaders.

6. The Pressures of Friendship

Last session we discussed friendship and how friends behave towards each other. Sometimes friends put pressure on us to do something which we don't really agree with and we feel is not right. By "right" we usually mean responsible, what others in society expect from us, our moral duty as members of a community.

Our parents and others in authority usually try to teach us a sense of what is the right thing to do. To say "yes" to the right way, however, may mean saying "no" to friendship, at least temporarily. Hence, we feel a conflict inside us.

7. Moral Dilemmas

Take these situations for group discussion.

Situation 1: You are in a shop with your friend. You see him steal a pen and put it in his pocket.

How do you feel?

What could you do? Is this COOL/WEAK/AGGRO?
What could your friend do? Is this COOL/WEAK/AGGRO?

What would be the consequences of each solution?

Consider the long and short term consequences.
Is it a FRIENDLY thing to do?
What do you think is the RIGHT or responsible thing for you/your friend to do?

Is there a clear right or wrong answer? Does it depend on the consequences as well as other considerations like how expensive is the item stolen, or how long you have been friends?

Situation 2: Some of your friends are having fun pulling a public telephone to pieces. They want you to join in. They call you "chicken".

Repeat the above steps for group discussion.

Do you feel the same way about all types of vandalism?

Situation 3: Your parents let you sleep over with a group at your friends' place. Their parents are out. Your friend has bought some drugs and urges everyone to rage.

Discuss as above.

Do you feel the same about all types of drugs, alcohol and tobacco included?

The point to emphasize about such moral dilemmas — friendship imposes pressures which effect our evaluation of solutions and consequences. Sometimes we must weigh the friendship on one hand and doing what we think is the right thing on the other hand. Sometimes the RIGHT way may not be the FRIENDLY way, at least in the short term. Well, is the RIGHT way the COOL way because you are standing up for yourself and what you believe in? Or can the right way be WEAK, or AGGRO? Discuss as relevant to the sophistication and maturity of the group.

8. Homework

A dilemma regarding the right thing to do and the pressures of friendship.

9. Leaders' Meeting

Following the session, leaders from parent and adolescent groups meet to discuss progress and evaluate goals.

SOLVING PROBLEMS THE RIGHT WAY

You are allowed to have a party at your place provided you don't make a mess and there is no alcohol. Your parent (s) go out for a while during the party leaving you in charge. While they are out and the party is going well, a few other friends arrive. They bring some alcohol. Soon they get a bit rough with the furniture and take your father's special port out of the cupboard. You don't want to upset your friends but you do feel responsible to your parents.

1. What is a WEAK way of handling this problem? _____

   What might the consequence be? _____

   _____

2. What is an AGGRO way? _____

   What might the consequence be? _____

   _____

3. What is a COOL way? _____

   What might the consequence be? _____

   _____

4. What is a FRIENDLY way? _____

   Why? _____

   _____

5. What do you think is the RIGHT thing to do? _____

   _____

   Is this COOL/WEAK/AGGRO? _____

   Why? _____

   Is this a FRIENDLY way? _____

   Why? _____

   _____

SOCIAL SKILLS TRAINING PROGRAMME FOR YOUNG ADOLESCENTS
SESSION 8: GROUP PROBLEM SOLVINGTHE CO-OPERATIVE WAY

Aims of Session 8

- to discuss the notion that we all belong to groups; social, sporting, family, school.
- to illustrate that for groups to function, especially when making decisions or performing tasks for the benefit of the group, individual members need to co-operate with each other.
- to demonstrate the helpful and unhelpful roles people assume during group decision making.
- to demonstrate that the CO-OPERATIVE way in group problem solving is often the FRIENDLY way and the COOL way (speaking up for yourself while considering and respecting others).
- to apply this concept to the planning of a farewell party.

Materials Required

- attendance chart, STOP-THINK-DO and COOL/WEAK/AGGRO posters, paper, textas
- video camera and monitor (optional)
- for Group Discussion and Roleplay

		7 cards (about 10 x20 cm) each with a role named and instructions regarding how to play the part
The Leader	—	starts the discussion
		organizes and summarizes the different ideas expressed
		keeps others on the topic in a helpful way
The Clown	—	mucks around
		distracts others
		makes others laugh
The Yes Man	—	praises people for their ideas
		agrees with others rather than giving own ideas
		asks everyone else what they think in a friendly way
The Loudmouth	—	talks too much and doesn't listen
		interrupts others
		constantly changes the subject
The Cop Out	—	does not join in at all
		quiet
		switched off
The Ideas Man	—	offers information and ideas to help the discussion along
		enthusiastic about new ideas
The Put Down	—	pays out others, hurts their feelings
		puts down their ideas and suggestions
		embarrasses others and makes them feel silly

homework for week 8 affixed during the session

Procedure

1. Review last session
   - the pressures of friendship
   - to decide what is the RIGHT (responsible) thing to do, you need to evaluate possible consequences, short and long term, of your decision.
2. Record points for attendance and homework completion
3. A Personal and Moral Dilemma

   Break into 2 smaller groups to discuss homework exercise.

   Note the difficulty in choosing a solution which is
   - COOL (standing up firmly and positively for yourself)
   - FRIENDLY (fair, considerate and loyal to your friends, including the rougher ones)
   - RIGHT (morally responsible to your parents and the parents of your friends)
4. Group Problem Solving

   Return to large group. We all belong to a number of different groups in our life. Ask children to list the groups they belong to — social, sporting, school, family. For groups to function properly, the individual people in the group cannot always have their own way or there would be continual conflict and the group would fall apart. Recall in the first session of the Social Skills Group, rules were made which were fair to everyone. If we had not co-operated with these rules, at least most of the time, the group would not have been able to work as it has. Co-operation is the key for groups to function properly.
5. Group Discussion Roleplay

   Group forms a circle. Each person is handed a card with a role description outlined (see above for description). Leave at least one person to act as observer, and comment on the success or otherwise of the group's decision making attempts and on the relative helpfulness of various members.

   Present the group with a topic for discussion e.g.

   > This group has been given $20 for being the most effective group this year. Decide together how to spend the money.

   > The group has been shouted to a special outing but you have to all go together. Decide where you want to go.

   > In order to get the concession fare for this outing, the group has to have a name. Decide what you should be called.

   Encourage each member to act out their part convincingly during the discussion. After a while, stop the discussion and ask for input from the observer about the helpfulness of various roles in the decision making process. Reinforce the idea that the group was not meant to be successful in reaching a decision because of the destructive roles some people were playing.

   Shuffle parts around and introduce a new topic with another observer until all members have had the opportunity of playing a helpful and an unhelpful part.

   Some roleplays may be videotaped and discussed more fully on playback.

6. Personal Feedback

Following this exercise, ask the group to assess the role each of the members usually takes in regular group discussions. Also note whether there have been changes in the usual roles individuals assume from early sessions of the group until now.

7. Break (10 minutes)

Refreshments, conversation and an opportunity to informally discuss diary entries with each other and/or leaders.

8. Group Problem Solving Applied

Planning a farewell party and activities.

Pose questions such as

— what tasks need doing.
— what things are to be brought from home.
— what activities are to be arranged.
— who is responsible for what.

Have children list suggestions on paper. A group member may be elected to co-ordinate planning.

Comment on the helpful or unhelpful roles individuals play in this group problem solving exercise.

Reinforce CO-OPERATIVE decision making.

Encourage members to make commitments in terms of specific tasks or activities and what items to bring from home.

Emphasize that behaving in a CO-OPERATIVE way in group decision making and group activities requires COOL and FRIENDLY behaviour from the individuals — speaking up for themselves and giving their own ideas while still being considerate of others' ideas.

9. Homework

An interpersonal problem to solve — saying goodbye

Personal commitment to a group decision.

GROUP PROBLEM SOLVING THE CO-OPERATIVE WAY

1. Next session we say goodbye to the group.

   How do you feel? _____

   What do you want to happen? _____

2. What can you do about it? _____

   _____

   _____

3. What have you gained from coming to the group? _____

   _____

   _____

   _____

4. Has coming to the group helped you at home? _____

   How? _____

   How has the parent attending the parent group helped you achieve your goals? _____

   _____

5. Has coming to the group helped you at school? _____

   How? _____

   How has your teacher helped you achieve your goals? _____

   _____

6. How could we improve the group programme for future groups? _____

   _____

7. Next session is also our farewell party. If we all co-operate then we will all enjoy it.

   What have you promised to bring?_____

   _____

   What activities or tasks have you agreed to help with? _____

SOCIAL SKILLS TRAINING PROGRAMME FOR YOUNG ADOLESCENTS
SESSION 9: SAYING GOODBYE

Aims of Session 9
- to encourage the farewell party as a co-operative group exercise.
- to evaluate goal achievement for the adolescents in the group.
- to determine the generalization of positive outcomes to school and home.
- to discuss the issue of saying goodbye.

Materials Required
- attendance chart, STOP-THINK-DO and COOL/WEAK/AGGRO posters, textas, paper
- goal sheets completed in earlier weeks fixed on walls. Include the children's comments from session 1 on why they are attending the group and what they hope to achieve; friendliness sheets from session 6; notes from teacher feedback in session 4.
- furniture, equipment, decorations for party.
- Self Report Forms: POST GROUP (Appendix 13) and pens.

Procedure
1. Review last session.
   - groups can only function when all members co-operate — then all feel okay. Recall the destructive effects of some roles on group discussion and decision making.
   - relate this to planning of farewell activities.
2. Record points for attendance and homework completion on chart.
3. Personal Feedback Regarding Change

   Have sheets of paper on the floor, each with a child's name on. Ask all children to record on each sheet the changes they feel that person has made in the group.

   Save these sheets for reference in Review session.
4. Review Group Goals

   Discuss these comments regarding change in the light of goals identified earlier in the group. Compare the children's comments for homework after the first session with those recorded in homework for last session, using the following questions:—

   "Have you achieved your goals in the group?"

   "Has this helped you achieve goals at school and at home?"

   Discuss the generalization of skills learned in the group to these other environments.

   "How have the parents who are attending the parent group helped you achieve your goals?"

   "What will your parents say about your progress?"

   "How have your teachers helped you achieve your goals?"

   "What will your teachers say about your progress?"

   Record the children's comments for discussion with parents and teachers in the following week.

   "Are there any other goals you would like to achieve?"

115

5. Self Report Forms: POST GROUP completed by adolescents.

6. Diary Entries

   Discuss diary entries volunteered by children. Encourage discussion using STOP-THINK-DO method and evaluation according to COOL/WEAK/AGGRO, FRIENDLY & RIGHT criteria or effective group problem-solving criteria where applicable.

7. Farewell Party

   Children take the responsibility of running the party e.g. when to eat, when to have activities, who will do what and when, cleaning up.

8. Goodbyes

   Group comes together to say goodbye. Encourage sharing of feelings about saying goodbye and ideas on what they can do about it e.g. exchange telephone numbers, addresses to keep in contact. Ask also for suggestions on how to improve the group programme for future groups of young people. Remind them of review session in 3 months.

9. Post Group Teacher Involvement

   Following this session, group leaders initiate post group contact with the teachers involved in the programme (see Chapter 6).

SOCIAL SKILLS TRAINING PROGRAMME FOR YOUNG ADOLESCENTS
POST GROUP: EVALUATION

Aims

- to collate information received from teachers, parents, adolescents and group leaders regarding the progress of the adolescents over the term of the group.
- to plan the feedback to parents in the following week.
- to check the viability of recommendations for further management.

Materials Required

- completed forms (PRE GROUP) and (POST GROUP) from parents, teachers and adolescents (self).
- goal achievement sheets completed in session 9 of the adolescent group.
- Social Skills Programme Evaluation Forms (Appendix 15).

Procedure

1. Following session 9 and the return of the teacher forms, leaders of the adolescent and parent groups meet to evaluate progress and goal achievement for the adolescents and parents in the training programme.

2. Rating Scales Evaluation

   a) Compare the ratings from the PRE and POST group assessments obtained from parents, teachers and adolescents on the various scales reflecting social competence and social skills deficits. Specifically, a comparison of the PRE and POST ratings will reflect trends or changes in:—

      peer acceptance

      attention seeking behaviour

      aggressiveness (physical and verbal)

      self-confidence

      ability to cope with teasing

      maturity

      ability to make and keep friends.

   b) Compare also the relative strengths and weaknesses of these trends from the various significant viewpoints monitored during the term of the training programme (parents, teachers, adolescents, group leaders).

3. Goal Achievement

   Assess goal achievement from the various viewpoints. Include an assessment of the goals achieved by the parents attending the parent group.

4. Recommendations.

   Suggestions for further management may include

   — follow-up involvement in social skills training programme for "booster" sessions.

   — referral to local resources or community groups e.g. youth organizations, community health clinic, Education Department resource (or equivalent in private school system).

   — referral for specialist input if specific problems have been identified in the group e.g.

specific learning difficulty, co-ordination problems, hearing difficulties, possible organic dysfunction, marital problems, sexual abuse.

5. Prepare summaries for feedback to parents in session 10 (refer to Parent Training Programme, session 10).

6. Written Reports

Following session 10, the leaders of the adolescent group complete Social Skills Programme Evaluation Reports on the adolescents for whom they are responsible in the group. These reports are made available to parents, teachers and the referring persons.

SOCIAL SKILLS TRAINING PROGRAMME FOR YOUNG ADOLESCENTS
REVIEW: MAINTENANCE AND GENERALIZATION

Aims of Review Session

- to renew acquaintances.
- to evaluate goal maintenance over 3 month period for adolescents in the group.
- to evaluate generalization of positive outcomes over school and home environments and different social situations.
- to make further recommendations for management and goal attainment.

Materials Required

- large sheets of paper, textas
- goal achievement sheets completed during the final group session fixed on the wall
- Self Report Forms: REVIEW (Appendix 14) and pens
- refreshments

Procedure

1. Renew acquaintances

    Discuss contacts maintained between the people in the group. Discuss feelings about this meeting compared with the first group session.

2. Maintenance of Goals

    Refer children to the goals set and achieved during the term of the group. Check whether they have maintained the goals they achieved. Record their responses. Discuss what they might do to re-establish their goals if they have not been maintained. Use a STOP-THINK-DO approach to this problem and encourage all children to participate in discussions. Additionally, check if children have new goals which they would like to achieve.

    Discuss how they might achieve these goals.

3. Self Report Forms: REVIEW completed by adolescents.

4. Refreshments and Informal Discussion

    One leader remains with the group to participate in conversation while the other leader joins the parent group to discuss the children for whom they have taken responsibility. They exchange roles half-way through the session.

5. Parent Feedback

    A leader from the adolescent group joins the parent group to

    — discuss progress of adolescents in the group in social areas particularly related to the home, and the maintenance of goals achieved in the group. Check over the information provided by the children and parents in their REVIEW forms.

    — discuss the teachers' comments regarding progress and their ratings of the adolescents on the REVIEW forms.

    — make recommendations for future management.

6. Final Note

    A brief report on progress is made to the persons who initially referred the young people to the Social Skills training programme.

Chapter 5
Parent
Training Programme

Chapter 5:
Parent Training Programme

OUTLINE

Aims of Session 1:
- to get to know parents in the group
- to provide information regarding the child/adolescent social skills programme
- to provide information regarding the parent programme and teacher involvement
- to encourage regular attendance
- to identify parents' goals for group attendance for themselves and their children
- to develop a supportive, trusting group environment

Materials Required
- blank name tags
- attendance chart
- Parent Forms: PRE GROUP (Appendix 5) and pens
- STOP-THINK-DO posters (Appendix 18)
- Handouts on Overview of Communication and Problem Solving Strategies (Appendix 22)
- Observation of Behaviour Exercise (Appendix 23)
- homework sheets for session 1
- refreshments

Procedure
Issue blank name tags to leaders and parents for first name to be placed on tags.

1. Initial Contact
    Leaders introduce themselves to parents, including information about their experience and interest in such programmes. Parent Forms: PRE GROUP completed. On these forms, parents
    - rate the children on various dimensions of social behaviour and skill, e.g. peer acceptance, attention seeking or withdrawn behaviours and maturity. They also describe positive features of the children.
    - specify goals for the children and themselves to achieve during the training programme. Group leaders may need to explain what is meant by goals for achievement with examples.
    - provide consent for video taping the children in the group.
    - provide consent for leaders from the child/adolescent group to visit teachers at school to enlist their support in the training programme, and (for 7 — 12 year olds) obtain ratings of acceptance by school peers in their natural environment.

    If further explanation of the forms is required, refer to Chapter 2.

2. Parent Introductions
    For parents to become acquainted with each other, they are formed into pairs for joint interviews. Information is gained from each other regarding hobbies, occupation, and interests, with the emphasis on the parent and not the child. Parents then report to the

group at least two (2) items of information about the parent they interviewed.

3. Attendance

Record parents' attendance on the Attendance Chart. Discuss the importance of regular attendance, to ensure that essential concepts are not missed by the children or parents. Mention that children receive rewards for maintained attendance. If a charge has been made for involvement in the programme, a partial refund for regular attendance may be discussed.

4. Sessional Details

Although mentioned in the Invitation to Attend, remind parents that sessions are held over 10 weeks, with 9 sessions for their children. The tenth session is a feedback session for parents conducted with leaders from both parent and child groups to evaluate progress at the completion of the programme.

Extra after hours sessions are scheduled for the second and seventh weeks for spouses/caregivers who are unable to attend the weekly sessions. They attend together with the regular group members. The purpose of these sessions is to provide information to these individuals regarding the group programme and to enlist the support of significant others in the home environment. Suggest a tentative date for the first spouse/caregiver session, and request parents to check the suitability of this time, to be confirmed in session 2. Parents are requested to be punctual for all sessions.

Advise parents of training sessions to be held in week 3 and 6 for the teachers of the children whose parents have given permission for teacher involvement in the programme. The aims of these sessions are to train teachers in the principles and methods utilized in the child/adolescent and parent programmes, and to enlist teacher support to assist transfer of social skills acquired in the group into the school setting.

5. An Introduction to the Child/Adolescent Social Skills Programme

Provide information and open discussion on the specified aims of the social skills training programme, the format of sessions and the rules for behaviour in the group to ensure adequate behaviour management (refer to session 1 of the child or adolescent programme).

Discuss the major components of the child/adolescent programme including the identification of specific personal and interpersonal goals for achievement during the group and the STOP-THINK-DO problem solving method. Acquiring skills in solving their own social problems will assist the children in achieving the goals identified. Introduce the problem solving method briefly, using the traffic light motto displayed in poster form as follows:—

STOP   Reminds the children to STOP before acting, consider the problem, decide how they and others feel, and the goals they wish to attain in that situation.

THINK   Reminds the children to THINK about many possible solutions, and to consider the consequences of each solution.

DO   Reminds the children to choose the best solution, with the most acceptable consequences for those involved, and DO it. Return to STOP and repeat the process if the chosen solution is not effective.

This method will be described to parents in more detail in session 3.

Homework is another important component of the programme for both children and parents. Children will be encouraged to attempt homework and return their homework books or diaries each session. Stress that children's homework is their responsibility.

6.   Refreshments

Provide a break with refreshments to contribute to informality and conversation.

7.   Introduction to the Parent Training Programme

Outline the specific aims of the parent programme and the general format of the group sessions (refer to Chapter 2 for details).

Explain that the basic concepts and techniques which will be taught in the programme will complement those presented in the child/adolescent group, with tailoring to fit the family environment.

Issue the handouts on Overview of Communication and Problem Solving Strategies to which parents may refer during the course to determine where specific concepts and techniques fit within the overall programme.

Major components include communication skills development, such as active listening to children and appropriate expression of feelings and ideas; the concept of problem ownership as a basis for deciding which strategies or techniques are best to use in a given situation; the STOP-THINK-DO problem solving approach for handling social conflicts within and outside the family situation; and the fostering of responsibility taking by children for solving their own problems. Relevant examples of these concepts may be discussed. Parents of children in the 7 — 12 year group may participate in problem solving exercises in the child group from session 5 onwards. This is not suitable for the adolescent programme.

Parents receive formal homework exercises to supplement the learning and practice of concepts and methods presented in the weekly sessions. Urge parents to attempt the exercises which also aid reinforcement and generalization of the programme content presented to the children each week.

Emphasize that the leaders' role in the parent programme is to present material and facilitate discussion. Suggest that parents utilize the material they find helpful. As the leaders are not experts, issues and questions are referred to the group for discussion. It may be necessary to reiterate the role of group leaders throughout the term.

8.   Problem and Goal Identification

Invite parents to describe the social difficulties of the children, and behavioural problems experienced at school and/or home. This discussion heightens parents' awareness of others experiencing similar problems.

Following from this discussion, and from responses on the Parent Forms, identify goals that parents would like their children and themselves to achieve by participating in the programme. This aids in planning appropriate management strategies for alleviating the social and behavioural problems identified. Record the information for discussion with leaders of the child/adolescent group.

9.   Understanding Behaviour by Observation

The first step for parents in managing or assisting their children to manage their social and behavioural problems involves closely observing what actually occurs and determining the need or purpose the behaviour serves. In this session, focus is on accurate observation of behaviour. The following questions are considered when observing behaviour:—

- What the child/adolescent did
- Parent's feelings.
- Parent's reaction.
- Child's response.

To demonstrate the use of these categories, group leaders roleplay the following parent-child situation. Distribute Observation of Behaviour Exercise for parents to follow:— •

Parent	(friendly tone):	*"Hi, how was school today?"*
Child	(sounding dejected):	*"Oh, alright I suppose".*
Parent		*"What happened?"*
Child		*"The teacher's given us heaps of homework, and I can't do it all. It's not fair. I'm not going to do it all. There's too much".*
Parent	(in angry tone):	*"Your marks aren't that good. You'd better get into your room right now and get started on it or you'll be up all night doing it."*
Child		*"Ah it's not fair. I don't want to do it".*
Parent		*"You get in there now, off you go."*

Child reluctantly goes to room.

Parents discuss the situation using the questions on the handout.

— What the child/adolescent did

   Refused to do homework

— Parent's feeling.

   Angry, worried.

— Parent's reaction

   Bossed the child

— Child's response

   Submitted reluctantly; dawdled to room.

10. Homework

    Distribute homework sheets requiring parents to perform the above exercise with examples of their children's misbehaviour and appropriate behaviour observed at home during the week.

    Indicate that the purposes of misbehaviour will be discussed next session.

11. Collect name tags.

UNDERSTANDING SOCIAL BEHAVIOUR PROBLEMS

During this week, look for:—

1. One example of misbehaviour, and analyse it using the following headings:—

What the Child did   _____

                            _____

Your Feelings   _____

                            _____

Your Reactions   _____

                            _____

Child's Response   _____

                            _____

2. One example of positive/appropriate behaviour and analyse it using the following
    headings:—

What the Child did   _____

                            _____

Your Feelings   _____

                            _____

Your Reactions   _____

                            _____

Child's Response   _____

                            _____

PARENT TRAINING PROGRAMME
SESSION 2: ATTENDING, LISTENING AND IDENTIFYING FEELINGS

Aims of Session 2:

- to promote an understanding of the purposes of misbehaviour.
- to discuss communication skills including attending behaviours, and the identification and expression of feelings.
- to facilitate the transfer of skills learned in session 2 of the child/adolescent group, specifically attending and listening skills which aid in the recognition of feelings in social situations.

Materials Required

- name tags
- attendance chart
- Purposes of Misbehaviour poster (Appendix 20)
- homework sheets for session 2
- refreshments

Procedure

Issue name tags

Record attendance

Confirm spouse/caregiver session to be held after hours in the forthcoming week.

1. Review Discussion

   The accurate observation and analysis of behaviour is the first step in understanding behaviour, prior to attempts to modify it or facilitate change by the child.

   Discuss the homework examples of observations of misbehaviour and appropriate behaviour provided by group members.

   Provide encouragement for attempting the exercise.

2. Goal Identification

   In a supportive manner, clarify parents' goals for group attendance concentrating particularly on goals for **themselves**.

   Record responses for display in the group room and write them on cards for parents to keep with them, enabling continual monitoring of progress towards goal attainment.

3. Information on the Child/Adolescent programme

   Report on the completion of school visits for teacher input into the assessment of the children's social difficulties and for school peer ratings of social acceptance (7 — 12 year olds).

   Session 2 of the child programme focusses on attending behaviours i.e. looking and listening to others to accurately observe what is happening around them so that they may interpret messages from others. This is also the method for recognizing feelings in themselves and others. In the adolescent group, the causal link between feelings and behaviour is discussed in depth.

   Provide an opportunity for parents to question or comment about the session content as presented.

126

4. Understanding the Purposes of Misbehaviour

The second step for parents in modifying or assisting their children to modify behaviour is to identify the purposes or goals of misbehaviour observed in particular situations. This will identify the benefits children expect to receive for behaving in certain ways.

Four purposes of misbehaviour have been conceptualized by Dreikurs (1972). Refer to poster. These include:—

- to gain attention
- to gain power
- to seek revenge
- to show inadequacy

Present the following problem situations. Before identifying the purposes of misbehaviour in each situation, analyze the situation and behaviour according to the questions posed last session:—

What did the child do?

What were the parent's feelings?

What was the parent's reaction?

What was the child's response?

Situation 1: (for 7 — 12 year olds)

Parent and child are walking past a vending machine containing packed sweets. The child asks for a packet. The parent reasons with the child that they are more expensive bought from a vending machine and that she cannot have a packet of sweets.

The child reacts with loud protestation and refusal to co-operate or move.

The parent gives in and buys the sweets.

Situation 2: (for adolescents)

A mother and daughter are shopping for some new clothes. Daughter chooses a pair of jeans and a jumper to wear to a party. The parent, on the other hand, wants her to buy a dress. They argue, and eventually the mother permits her daughter to purchase her choice.

Discuss these situations using the questions presented.

Explain that the purpose of the child's misbehaviour is 'power', which is shown actively by being unco-operative and argumentative, with the parent feeling angry and reacting by giving in to the child.

Situation 3:

It is the beginning of a new school year. The child indicates to the parent that he is worried about the location of classrooms, the teacher and harder schoolwork. Parent offers to help by taking him to school on the first day.

Discuss, considering the questions provided. The purpose of the child's behaviour is to show 'inadequacy'. He feels unable to cope with demands of a new year at school. The parent attempts to provide support and probably feels anxious and unconfident about the child's future.

Situation 4:

A child fails to do one of her weekly jobs for which pocket money is given. Parent refuses to grant pocket money for that week. The child then steals money from her younger brother.

Discuss as above.

Explain the purpose of the child's misbehaviour is 'revenge' or 'getting back' at the parent for discontinuing pocket money. The parent in turn would probably feel hurt and angry with the child and may also want to retaliate on behalf of the younger sibling.

Situation 5:

There is a new baby in the family. The young school age child reverts to immature behaviour (e.g. babyish speech, wanting assistance with dressing, playing younger games). Mother reminds him that he is a 'big boy now' and the baby needs help because it is little.

Situation 6: (for adolescents)

The family has been invited to an engagement party. Everyone is ready to leave home but the adolescent has just finished showering, and is trying to decide what to wear. The parent reminds him of the time, and the need to 'get a move on'.

Discuss as above.

The misbehaviours described have the purpose of 'attention'. In situation 5, the parent reminds the child of his status in the family, and thus the expectations regarding his behaviour. In situation 6, the adolescent is dawdling, the parent is probably becoming annoyed and urges him to dress quickly.

5. Refreshments

6. Communication

To date, parents have learnt to accurately observe behaviour and analyze it according to its purpose. However, to deal effectively with problem situations in which misbehaviour occurs and at the same time, improve and maintain positive relationships, parents need to be able to communicate effectively with their children. Effective communication then, is the third step in modifying, or assisting children to modify problem social behaviour.

As the children/adolescents are learning in their session, careful attention and listening are prerequisites for effective communication and problem solving. Parents need to indicate to their children that they are being heard. By careful listening, parents are able to identify and feedback how their children feel in particular situations. This provides encouragement for children to 'open up' and begin to consider ways of solving problem situations.

Thus, there are four (4) parts to this communication process:—

• Attending behaviours
• Identifying feelings
• Feeding back or reflecting those feelings to children
• Maintaining open responses

This session deals with attending behaviours and identification of feelings in line with the child/adolescent programme. These elements of effective communication help develop a trusting and supportive relationship between parents and children.

Refer parents to the Overview of Communication and Problem Solving Strategies handout to indicate skill learning level at this stage.

7. Attending Behaviours

These refer to the verbal and non-verbal behaviours that people show to indicate that they are paying attention and listening to others. To demonstrate these aspects of communication, leaders roleplay a situation which indicates non-attending behaviour.

For example, while one leader introduces a topic, the other leader shows poor attention through non-verbal behaviour, e.g. fidgetting, avoiding eye contact, and other inappropriate gestures. Ask the group members to describe non-verbal behaviours which would indicate attention in that situation and demonstrate these (e.g. looking at the speaker, remaining still).

As an example of poor verbal attending behaviours, roleplay a situation in which one leader interrupts the other or asks questions unrelated to the topic. Ask group members to describe verbal behaviours that would indicate attention in that situation. Demonstrate these in the group. Verbal attending behaviours include prompts to encourage people to continue speaking e.g. "Mm, oh yes, tell me more". These indicate that the person is following the conversation and conveys acceptance of the speaker. Asking appropriate questions to check understanding of the content or to gain more information, as well as summarizing the content of the conversation are further examples of verbal attending behaviours.

8.   Identification of Feelings

Another aspect of the communication process is the identification of feelings. Provide examples of situations which convey feelings, using both verbal and non-verbal cues. Ask the group to identify the feeling indicated when the leader

— demonstrates a happy face
— uses an unsure, hesitant tone of voice and asks, "Do you think this is alright?"
— looks and says angrily, "It's not fair, you never let me go anywhere."
— says dejectedly, "I only got a C for my project. I don't think I'll pass this term now".

9.   Homework

Parents are encouraged to complete an exercise on observing and analyzing mis-behaviours, and the communication skills outlined in this session. The children will also have homework which requires the practice of attending behaviours and feeling identification.

Next session will focus on the two other aspects of the communication process, reflective listening including feedback of feelings, and the use of open reflective responses.

10.   Leaders' Meeting

Following the session, leaders of the parent group meet with leaders of the child group to discuss goals specified by participants in the groups, current concerns and progress.

Homework: Session 2
ATTENDING, LISTENING AND IDENTIFYING FEELINGS

1. Record and analyse one purpose of misbehaviour using the following questions:—

    What did the child do?   _____

                                                    _____

    How did you feel?   _____

                                                    _____

    What was your reaction?   _____

                                                    _____

    What was the child's response?   _____

                                                    _____

    What was the purpose of the
    misbehaviour? i.e. to gain or   _____
    display attention, power,
    revenge, inadequacy.   _____

2. Practice non-verbal and verbal attending behaviours.

3. Write one example of identifying your child's feelings.

    How did your child react?

    _____

    _____

    _____

4. Bring to the next session, topics you would like to discuss in future sessions.

PARENT TRAINING PRGRAMME
SESSION 2 (s): SPOUSE/CAREGIVER INVOLVEMENT

Aims of Session 2 (s):

- to provide information regarding the aims and content of the child/adolescent social skills and parent training programmes to spouses/caregivers who are unable to attend the weekly sessions.

- to present the critical concepts and techniques in the training programmes and allow for practice in the session.

- to encourage a broader base for the extension of learned social skills into the home environment through the support of significant others in the family.

Materials Required

- name tags
- handouts on Overview of Communication and Problem Solving Strategies. (Appendix 22)
- Observation of Behaviour Exercise (Appendix 23)
- Purposes of Misbehaviour poster (Appendix 20)
- printed examples for practice of open, reflective listening (refer session 3)
- STOP-THINK-DO, COOL/WEAK/AGGRO posters (Appendix 18, 19)
- STOP-THINK-DO Handouts for Parents (Appendix 25, 26)
- COOL/WEAK/AGGRO Handouts (Appendix 24)
- video of 'The Fight' from 'What Should I Do?' series. (Additional Resource Materials). If unavailable, provide a printed social interaction problem situation.
- video recorder and monitor
- blackboard, chalks or paper, textas
- refreshments

Procedure

Issue name tags.

Group leaders introduce themselves and invite introductions from spouses/caregivers.

Indicate the aims of this session as above.

1. Information on the Child/Adolescent Programme

    Provide a brief description of the social skills training programme for children with emphasis on specific aims, the format of each session and critical components such as goal setting and the problem solving method.

    Problem Solving Component

    Show the video which demonstrates the problem solving sequence in a social conflict situation.

    Distribute handouts on STOP-THINK-DO which outline the role of parents as mediators for their children in the problem solving process. They facilitate the child's acquisition of problem solving skills and their application in the home setting.

    Specifically, parents encourage their children to stop before behaving, consider the problem, how everyone feels and what they want to happen, think of possible solutions,

131

choose the most acceptable one and put it into action. Parents are also encouraged to use this approach themselves, not only to provide a powerful model for their child, but also to assist in the development of positive family relations based on effective communication and shared problem solving skills.

Strategy Evaluation Component

Another component of the child programme is the analyzing and evaluating of solutions or strategies according to the criteria of COOL/WEAK/AGGRO ways of behaving. Refer to the video for examples of each of these response styles. Distribute handouts.

Explain that the children in the group are encouraged to evaluate the consequences of ways of behaving in social situations. Since the COOL way generally has the most acceptable consequences, this is usually the best one to choose and try first.

Examples of the COOL way from the video include apologizing appropriately, standing up for oneself firmly but positively, walking away and doing something else. Compare this with the WEAK way (crying, telling tales) or the AGGRO way (fighting, abusing).

Goal Identification

Ask spouses/caregivers to describe their children's social and behavioural difficulties from their points of view, and to define the goals they would like the children to achieve by group attendance. Differences in perceived problems and goals between couples provide valuable information for leaders. Provide a progress report on children whose parents are present at the meeting. Indicate the goals identified to this point for each child in the group and that progress towards attainment will be regularly monitored by group leaders and group peers.

2. Refreshments

3. The Parent Training Programme

Emphasize that the programme for parents is complementary with the child programme.

Give a brief description of the aims and format of the parent programme (refer to chapter 2).

Distribute handouts on the Overview of Communication and Problem Solving Strategies and discuss the levels of skill learning outlined and thereby, the critical components of the parent programme. These include:

Problem ownership.

In a problem situation, it is important for parents to first decide who owns the problem to determine the strategies to use to solve it (if the parent has ownership) or to assist the child to solve it (if the child has ownership). Practice examples may be taken from sessions 5 & 6 of the parent programme.

Purposes of Misbehaviour.

Discuss the need to carefully observe behaviour and misbehaviour, and to analyze it in terms of the questions posed in the Observation of Behaviour Exercise and in terms of the purpose of the behaviour for the child. Refer to Purposes of Misbehaviour poster.

Communication Skills.

If parents are to solve problems they are having with their children or to assist the children to solve their own, there needs to be healthy parent-child relationships and a positive atmosphere for parent mediated or shared problem solving efforts. Communication skills are required to promote this atmosphere. Examples of these skills presented in the parent programme include attending behaviours (verbal and non-verbal), reflective listening, identification and feedback of feelings and appropriate use of I-messages. Present examples of these concepts from the relevant sessions.

Natural and Logical Consequences.

Stress the relevance of positive management strategies including encouragement and reinforcement of acceptable behaviour and efforts to practice newly acquired social skills, and the use of Natural and Logical Consequences applied to misbehaviour. Provide practical examples from the programme sessions.

4. Consistent Practice

Encourage spouses/caregivers to discuss concepts and techniques with those who are attending the weekly sessions, and to practice techniques at home with their children. This offers a more consistent parental approach for communicating and problem solving at home. The maintenance and generalization of developing skills in these areas will be enhanced.

5. Follow Up Session

Offer spouses/caregivers a further after hours session in week 7 to consolidate learning from this session and provide further feedback regarding the children's goal achievement. Arrange a date and time.

SESSION 3: REFLECTING FEELINGS AND SOLVING SOCIAL PROBLEMS

Aims of Session 3

- to present and practice open, reflective listening.
- to discuss STOP-THINK-DO problem solving approach in detail.
- to provide feedback to parents on the progress of their children in the group.
- to facilitate the transfer of skills learned in session 3 of the child/adolescent group, specifically recognition and reflection of feelings, the causes of feelings, and the problem solving process.

Materials Required

- name tags
- attendance chart
- printed examples to practice open, reflective listening
- STOP-THINK-DO posters (Appendix 18)
- STOP-THINK-DO Handouts for Parents (Appendix 25, 26)
- video of "The New Girl" from the "What Should I Do?" series; if unavailable, a printed example of a problem interaction situation.
- video recorder and monitor
- blackboard, chalks or paper and textas
- homework sheets for session 3
- refreshments

Procedure

Record attendance on chart.

1. Review Discussion.

    Using homework exercises, review the purposes of misbehaviour, verbal and non-verbal attending behaviours and the identification of feelings. Refer comments and questions from parents to the group for discussion. Record the topics which parents would like to discuss in future sessions.

2. Information on the Child/Adolescent Programme.

    Discuss with parents the comments made by leaders of the child/adolescent group at the leaders' meeting, regarding the children's progress in the group and their goals for achievement. Encourage parents to give feedback from their viewpoint on their children's progress in the programme.

    The focus of the child programme in session 3 is on the labelling of feelings and the identification of reasons for feelings ("Why did she feel like that? Because .... happened.") The adolescent group will also cover the STOP-THINK-DO problem solving method.

    A further focus for the child/adolescent group is the setting and reinforcement of personal and interpersonal goals within the supportive group environment. Examples of these goals include listening to others, speaking up for self, sharing tasks, behaving sensibly.

The specific goals identified for each child will be discussed in the parent group next week, following the teacher training session in which goals in the school setting will be clarified.

3. Reflective Listening.

Review the 4 parts of the communication process.

— Attending behaviour
— Identifying feelings
— Feeding back or reflecting these feelings to the child
— Maintaining open responses

This session deals with reflective listening and open communication. Reflective listening refers to feeding back to the child how he/she feels about a particular situation in a manner which opens up the communication between speaker and listener.

The open response indicates that the listener has heard and understood the feelings behind the speaker's words. A closed response indicates that the listener has not heard and understood the feelings behind the speaker's words. Leaders roleplay situations which exemplify open or closed reflective listening.

Situation 1.

Child: "Mum, Steven won't let me watch The Addams Family. He never lets me watch any of my favourite T.V. shows".

Parent: "You feel angry with Steven for not letting you watch your favourite programme".

This is an example of an open response as the parent has heard and understood the child's feeling, and reflected it back to the child.

Child: "Steven won't let me watch The Addams Family. He never lets me watch any of my favourite T.V. shows."

Parent: "You can't have your own way all the time".

This is a closed response. The parent has ignored the child's feelings of anger and disappointment, and is indicating that he/she does not want to hear about the child's problem.

Situation 2.

Adolescent
(excitedly): "I passed my Science Exam. I got a B for it".

Parent: "Oh, did you?"

Indicate that this is an example of a closed response, and discuss reasons with group members.

Adolescent
(excitedly): "I passed my Science Exam. I got a B for it".

Parent: "You're really pleased (happy, excited,) with your science mark".

Discuss this open response example with group members.

4. Group Practice Activities.

Handout the following list of child and parent statements giving open and closed responses to each. Firstly, ask parents to decide if responses are open or closed and secondly, construct open, reflective listening responses from closed responses. Emphasize to parents that in the construction of open responses, they listen and look for the feelings conveyed and express them in words.

Discuss responses after each practice item.

Child/Adolescent's Statement.	Parent's Response.
"I wanted to go out with my friends. You're the most unfair parent in the world".	"I told you you couldn't go out with them and that's final."
"I can't do any of this maths. It's stupid".	"You're worried about understanding the maths".
"See what I painted today at school".	"Yes it's nice".
"Mum, Jodie's asked me to go to the pictures with her, but I promised I'd go to Kelly's house then".	"Actually I don't think you should go to either. You've been out enough this week".

As a further exercise, divide the group into pairs to practice giving and receiving open reflective listening responses using the following list of child/adolescent statements.

(angrily), "You couldn't understand me. You're too old".

(excitedly), "Look at my new model".

"I don't want to go to bed. It's too early".

"Why can't we have video games, everyone else at school has them?"

"Mum/Dad where are my footy boots?"

"I have to finish my project tonight and I haven't any pictures".

"I don't have to do it if I don't want to".

If further practice is required, refer to the list of excellent child statements in the Appendix (pp 307-309) in Parent Effectiveness Training by Dr. Thomas Gordon (1970).

5. Refreshments.

6. The STOP-THINK-DO Problem Solving Approach in Detail

Accurately identifying feelings and reflecting them back for checking by the other person indicates that the person is being heard and understood. It also opens the door for the person with the problem to begin to search for solutions. This provides the link between communication skills and problem solving skills. Reflective listening is a major component of the problem solving process and is involved specifically at the STOP stage when the problem is first considered and feelings identified, and in the THINK stage when proposed solutions are evaluated in terms of how the person feels about the likely consequences of each strategy.

Show the video and using the traffic light motto, discuss the STOP-THINK-DO approach to solving the social problem depicted in the film.

Pose the questions:—

What is the problem?

How does each person in the situation feel?

What do you think each person would want to happen?

What could each person do to solve the problem?

What might be the consequences of each strategy?

What is the best choice, i.e. the one with the most acceptable consequences for all concerned?

If this does not work out, STOP and THINK about something else to do.

Refer to session 4 of the child group or session 3 of the adolescent group for a comprehensive presentation of the STOP-THINK-DO process in relation to the film, "The New Girl".

If a video is unavailable, describe or roleplay a social conflict situation and pose the questions as above. Suggested problem situations follow:—

For 7 — 12 year olds:

Tom and Bob are playing with their radio controlled cars. Tom's car is bigger than Bob's and when it hits Bob's car, it crushes it hard against the wall. The front bumper bar of Bob's car is smashed, and he runs toward Tom's car to try to smash it. Tom tries to stop him and a fight starts.

For adolescents:

Helen and Jan sit near each other in maths. Helen is often in trouble with her teacher for disruptive behaviour and has been threatened with suspension. Jan excitedly leans over to tell her about her terrific weekend while the teacher is occupied. However, she hears chatter and mistakenly chastizes Helen, sending her to the Head Office. Jan says nothing. Helen glares at her and mutters "I'll get you for this!"

For further examples of conflict situations, refer to the homework exercises in session 4 of the child and adolescent programmes.

Distribute the STOP-THINK-DO Problem Solving handouts to parents. These trace the role of parents as mediators or facilitators, assisting and guiding children in the problem solving process. The relevance of feeling identification and reflection is indicated.

7.   Homework.

A reflective listening exercise is set.

Encourage parents to refer to the STOP-THINK-DO Problem Solving handout and to follow the steps in the mediation process when particular problems arise either between parent and child where the parent needs to find a solution or both parent and child do, or when the child has a problem to solve him/herself.

Next session will provide further practice in the STOP-THINK-DO method and the use of encouragement as reinforcement for new skills and attitudes. Remind parents that teachers will be attending for a training session during the forthcoming week.

REFLECTING FEELINGS AND SOLVING SOCIAL PROBLEMS

1. Practice using open, reflective listening during the week.

2. Write examples of open reflective listening below.

Child's/Adolescent's Statement   **Your Response**

1. _____   _____

     _____   _____

2. _____   _____

     _____   _____

3. _____   _____

     _____   _____

3. Describe a problem involving your child where you guided or assisted him/her to solve the problem with the STOP-THINK-DO method.

_____

_____

_____

_____

_____

_____

_____

4. How did you reflect back his/her feelings?

_____

_____

_____

_____

_____

_____

SESSION 4: ENCOURAGING SKILL ACQUISITION AND MAINTENANCE

Aims of Session 4

- to provide further practice of open, reflective listening.
- to provide practice of the STOP-THINK-DO problem solving method.
- to discuss the use of encouragement to reinforce newly acquired skills and positive social goal direction.
- to correlate goals formulated for the children in their group, home and school environments.
- to facilitate the transfer of skills training in session 4 of the child/adolescent group, specifically confidence in their own problem solving skills through practice and more refined evaluation of strategies and consequences.

Materials Required

- attendance chart
- video of "The Fight" from the "What Should I Do?" series, or printed examples of social interaction problem situations
- video recorder and monitor
- blackboard and chalks or paper and textas
- notes regarding specific goals for children as identified in the child/adolescent group and by teachers at the teacher training session
- homework sheets for session 4
- refreshments

Procedure

Record attendance on chart.

1. Review Discussion.

   Discuss with parents their examples of open, reflective listening. If further clarification is required, roleplay the homework examples. Refer questions from parents to the group for discussion. Encourage homework attempts as they are beneficial to aid understanding and application of concepts. Moreover, homework exercises are designed to reinforce instruction received by children.

2. Information on the Child/Adolescent Programme.

   Outline the specific goals set for the children from the discussions of group peers and leaders in the child/adolescent group. Indicate that these goals will be actively reinforced and monitored regularly within the supportive group environment. Suggest that parents may continue this support at home for goals and behaviours which are compatible with those identified by parents for the home environment.

   Additionally, outline goals in the school setting identified by teachers in the recent teacher training session. Discuss the compatibilty of goals set from different viewpoints and for various environments. Discuss also the plans of action made for skills development and goal attainment in the school situation through the mediation and assistance of teachers in the same way as has been suggested for parents. Encourage reinforcement from parents for these plans. Parent's may meet with teachers at school to discuss goals and ensure consistent management and mediating strategies for positively influencing social skills acquisition, transfer and maintenance for their children.

The children's session will focus on practicing social problem solving skills. Adolescents will refine their evaluation of suggested solutions to include the style of response (i.e. cool, weak, or aggro styles of responding).

3. STOP-THINK-DO Practice.

Revise the sequence of steps in the problem solving process, referring to the handout from the last session. Demonstrate the method using problem situations depicted in the parents' homework exercise.

One leader may take the parent role mediating in the problem solving process with the child, roleplayed by the parent who reported the particular problem situation. Discuss their responses according to the steps outlined in the STOP-THINK-DO handout. To facilitate discussion if parents are hesitant, show the video or provide written examples of problem situations and trace the steps specified in the handout.

4. Refreshments.

5. Encouragement.

Remind parents that using reflective listening opens up the communication between themselves and their children by showing that they are interested to hear about the children's views, feelings and activities. By using the STOP-THINK-DO approach with children, the parents also indicate confidence in their children and the belief that they are capable of solving their own problems. In using these techniques, parents need to utilize language which encourages children to maintain appropriate behaviours, including problem solving skills. Encouragement focusses on the children's appropriate on-going efforts to deal with situations, problem or otherwise.

Roleplay the following situation in which a group leader is a parent with a group member being a child.

The child's team has just lost a sports match. The parent is discussing the game in a critical manner with the child.

Following completion of the roleplay, ask the child for feedback regarding how he/she felt about the parent's statements.

Discuss with the group, and ask what the parent could say to be more encouraging.

Roleplay the situation again with the parent being encouraging to the child. Statements could include,

"How do you feel you played today?"

"You really tried hard to get into the game today".

Discuss with parents the language which they could use to encourage their children.

6. Discussion Topics.

Allow time for discussion of topics given by parents in Session 3. Relate these to concepts and techniques presented to date.

7. Homework.

A further exercise on reflective listening is set and examples of parents' use of encouragement are required.

Next session will focus on evaluating the solutions offered for problems in terms of COOL/WEAK/AGGRO criteria.

Problem ownership will also be discussed.

At the end of the session, a leader from the adolescent group informs parents about the arrangements for next session where adolescents will be encouraged to practice newly acquired skills in a natural environment. Parents, adolescents and group leaders will meet for lunch, followed by a parent session held in the usual venue.

Homework: Session 4
ENCOURAGING SKILL ACQUISITION AND MAINTENANCE

1. Practice using open, reflective listening.

    Write two (2) examples using open, reflective listening during this week.

    Child's Statement   **Your Response**

    1. _____   _____

        _____   _____

        _____   _____

    2. _____   _____

        _____   _____

        _____   _____

        _____   _____

        _____   _____

        _____   _____

2. Give an example of encouraging language you used with your child during the week.

    _____

    _____

    _____

    _____

    _____

    _____

    _____

SESSION 5: OWNING PROBLEMS AND CHOOSING COOL SOLUTIONS

Aims of Session 5

- to provide practice for STOP-THINK-DO problem solving approach.
- to present COOL/WEAK/AGGRO response styles as an abbreviated method for describing and evaluating solutions to social problem situations.
- to discuss the concept of Problem Ownership.
- to facilitate the transfer of skills learned in session 5 of the child/adolescent group, specifically the generation of problem solving strategies, consequential thinking and COOL behaviour patterns.

Materials Required

- attendance chart
- video "The Game" from "What Should I Do?" series, or printed example of a social interaction problem
- video recorder and monitor
- COOL/WEAK/AGGRO Handouts (Appendix 24)
- blackboard and chalks or paper and textas
- homework sheets for session 6
- refreshments

Procedure

Record attendance on chart.

1. Review Discussion.

   Review the concepts of open, reflective listening and the use of encouragement to promote positive communication between children and parents. Discuss homework exercises. If there is difficulty with understanding or applying these techniques provide opportunity for further practice.

2. Parent Goals

   Discuss the parents' goals for themselves in the group programme. Group members provide feedback to each other on their progress towards goal attainment, focussing on strengths and the skills requiring further practice.

3. Information on Child/Adolescent Programme.

   In the child group, session 5 focusses on COOL/WEAK/AGGRO ways of behaving to solve social problems. Two parents volunteer to join the child group for shared problem solving practice using these criteria. While adolescents are on their outing in a natural setting, they will also be encouraged to use these criteria to assess styles of behaving.

4. COOL/WEAK/AGGRO Response Styles.

   These terms are used to describe and evaluate the strategies or solutions suggested in the THINK stage of the STOP-THINK-DO process.

   Following the generation of solutions and consideration of likely consequences of these solutions, children are encouraged to decide if the behaviour required to execute each solution is indicative of a COOL (positively assertive), WEAK (passive) or AGGRO (aggressive) style of responding. These categories also aid in shortening the problem solving process once it has been well practiced since quick implications can be made regarding the likely consequences of strategies described in these terms. Distribute handouts on these response styles and discuss the verbal, non-verbal and emotional features of each response style.

Demonstrate these criteria using the following example of a customer who has paid the bill at a shop and has been short changed by the salesperson.

Roleplay 1. (Aggro Response Style)

Customer says *angrily*, "Hey, you've short-changed me. I gave you $5.00. You owe me $1.20. Where's your boss? I'll speak to him about this. I always have trouble when I shop here."

Roleplay 2. (Weak Response Style)
Customer looks at change, shrugs shoulders, and walks away.

Roleplay 3. (Cool Response Style)

Customer says in matter of fact tone, "Excuse me, I haven't received all my change. I gave you $5.00, and I ought to get back $1.20. Please check this for me".

Following each roleplay, ask parents to state which response style was portrayed, and give their reasons.

Emphasize that the COOL way generally has the most acceptable consequences for all involved and is therefore, a good solution to choose and try first.

5.   Practice in Problem Solving and Strategy Evaluation.

Present a social problem situation using a parent's example from the homework exercise, a problem solving video or group leader's examples to demonstrate the use of the STOP-THINK-DO approach, including COOL/WEAK/AGGRO descriptions of the strategies suggested.

Refer to session 5 (child group) and session 4 (adolescent group) for more information regarding the application of this approach in the social skills training programme and utilize the same method with the parent group. Record parent responses and discuss following the activity. As this material is being presented concurrently in the child programme, those parents who are observing the children's session will not miss these components of the programme.

Emphasize the need to encourage children to generate their own solutions. However if a child is not yet able, the parent continues to use open reflective listening. They may also suggest possible solutions and likely consequences in the initial stages of learning the process, while leaving the choice of solution to the child or adolescent.

If a child is hesitant to act on a choice, positive encouragement is provided by parents for even a small step towards problem solving. Initially another child or parent may be called on to model the behaviour for the child until confidence is gained.

6.   Refreshments.

Parents report back to the group on their observations in the children's session and the shared problem solving practice with their children.

Allow time for discussion of topics suggested by parents in session 3.

7.   Problem Ownership.

Refer parents to the handout on Overview of Communication and Problem Solving Strategies. To date, the parent programme has focussed on concepts and techniques which parents can use with their children when the children have a problem (for example open reflective listening and the STOP-THINK-DO problem solving method). In the remaining sessions, strategies will be presented which parents may use when they have problems with their children. Furthermore, by deciding "who owns the problem", parents are deciding the strategies they can use to solve parent problems or to assist their children in solving their own problems. Present Dr. Thomas Gordon's definition of problem ownership to the group.

This definition is as follows:—

1) "The child has a problem because he is thwarted in satisfying a need. It is not a problem for the parent because the child's behaviour in no tangible way interferes with the parent's satisfying his own needs. Therefore, THE CHILD OWNS THE PROBLEM.

2) The child is satisfying his own needs (he is not thwarted) and his behaviour is not interfering with the parent's own needs. Therefore, THERE IS NO PROBLEM IN THE RELATIONSHIP.

3) The child is satisfying his own needs (he is not thwarted). But his behaviour is a problem to the parent because it is interfering in some tangible way with the parent's satisfying a need of his own. NOW THE PARENT OWNS THE PROBLEM." P.64 (Refer to Additional Resource Materials).

Discuss the concept of problem ownership with group members, utilizing the following examples of child and parent problems:—

losing belongings at home.

late home from school and the family has planned to go shopping straight after school.

homework not completed.

untidy bedroom.

not doing jobs.

Group leaders may present parents' examples or include discussion topics suggested by parents if they are relevant to the concept of problem ownership.

8. Homework.

Exercises are presented on problem ownership and the problem solving method. Next session will pursue the concept of problem ownership and the practice of STOP-THINK-DO including COOL/WEAK/AGGRO response styles.

I-messages will be introduced for discussion.

9. Leaders' Meeting.

Following the completion of this session, leaders of the parent and child/adolescent groups meet to discuss concerns and progress towards goal attainment for the child and parent participants.

OWNING PROBLEMS AND CHOOSING COOL SOLUTIONS

1. Give an example of a problem situation in which you owned the problem.
   Provide an example of your child owning the problem.

   Parent Problem.

   _____

   _____

   Child Problem.

   _____

   _____

2. Use STOP-THINK-DO with your child during the forthcoming week.

   What happened? _____

   _____

   _____

   What did you do or say? _____

   Was that a COOL/WEAK/AGGRO way of behaving? _____

   What did your child do or say? _____

   _____

   Was that a COOL/WEAK/AGGRO way of behaving? _____

   _____

   Is STOP-THINK-DO a useful method for solving social problems?

   _____

SESSION 6: OWNING PROBLEMS AND FRIENDLY COMMUNICATION

Aims of Session 6

- to apply the concept of problem ownership to practice examples
- to practice the STOP-THINK-DO problem solving approach, including COOL/-WEAK/AGGRO response styles
- to present I-messages which communicate problem ownership and honest expression of feelings
- to provide feedback to parents on the progress of their children in the group
- to facilitate transfer of skills learned in session 6 by children/adolescents, specifically COOL and FRIENDLY ways of solving problems.

Materials Required.

- attendance chart
- video eg. "The Lunch Money", from the "What Should I Do?" series or a printed example of a social interaction problem
- video recorder and monitor
- blackboard and chalks or paper and textas
- homework sheets for session 6
- refreshments

Procedure

Record attendance on chart.

Enquire about interest in a further after hours session for spouses/caregivers in the seventh week. Remind parents of the date and time set previously.

1. Review Discussion.

   Review the concept of problem ownership and discuss the homework examples of child owned and parent owned problems.

   Ask parents to report on their application of the STOP-THINK-DO problem solving method to solve problems they had with their children or to assist their children in solving their own problems. Discuss the examples provided by parents in terms of the use of open, reflective listening. Ask parents to discuss the questions they ask their children in order to generate solutions and evaluate consequences. Encourage parents to trace the steps they and their children make towards problem solution.

   Refer parents' comments and questions to the group for discussion. Further examples of reflective listening and problem ownership may be presented if required.

2. Parent Goals.

   Discuss progress towards goal attainment for parents in the group, encouraging feedback from group members to each other.

3. Information on Child/Adolescent Programme.

   Enquire about progress from the parents' viewpoint of the children attending the group. Provide feedback about progress in the children's group as reported by the leaders of this group.

Session 6 in the child/adolescent programme focusses on further evaluation of strategies according to the COOL/WEAK/AGGRO criteria and also in terms of the FRIENDLY way of behaving. Children learn that to improve peer acceptance and to make friends, they need to behave like one. The FRIENDLY way of behaving is to show consideration of others and fairness to others in social situations. Children and adolescents will be practicing ways of handling negative or unfriendly behaviour, e.g., put downs and teasing.

Refer to session 6 in the child/adolescent programme for details and practice examples which may also be used in the parent programme.

4. Problem Solving and Strategy Evaluation Practice.

Two parents volunteer to join the children's session.

Parents form two groups. Ask for a parent example and discuss the concept of problem ownership and then utilize the STOP-THINK-DO problem solving sequence. Include an evaluation of the solutions proposed in terms of COOL/WEAK/AGGRO criteria, and also whether the solutions demonstrate FRIENDLY behaviours (showing consideration, fairness and respect for others in the situation).If parents are reluctant to offer examples for discussion, leaders provide problem situations or present a problem solving video to demonstrate application of the problem solving and strategy evaluation approach outlined. The group reforms following this activity to discuss the solution which is likely to have the most acceptable consequences for all those involved.

During the discussion, leaders comment on examples of the appropriate use by participants of techniques presented in previous sessions eg. attending behaviours, open, reflective listening and encouragement.

5. Refreshments.

Parents report back to the group on their problem solving practice in the child group using the FRIENDLY way criterion as well as the COOL/WEAK/AGGRO criteria for evaluating strategies and making quick implications about likely consequences.

Allow time for discussion of topics suggested by parents.

6. I-Messages.

Refer parents to handout on Overview of Communication and Problem Solving Strategies. I-messages assist parents in dealing with parent owned problems. Furthermore, because I-messages do not put down or convey negative judgements about the child, they show respect for children by parents.

Showing respect and consideration for another person is a FRIENDLY way to behave and communicate. You-messages are often put downs and negative statements which convey unfriendly messages.

To introduce I-messages, leaders roleplay a parent owned problem situation, assisted by parents eg. a child interrupts constantly while parents are engaged in conversation.

Roleplay 1 *(You-Message)*.

Parent angrily says: "Would you just stop that right now. You're always annoying me".

Roleplay 2 *(I-Message)*.

Parent says: "I find it hard to talk to your father when I get interrupted".

Parents discuss the roleplays, including the effect the messages would have on the 'child'. The You-message would probably make the child feel resentful and angry, and less likely to modify his/her behaviour. In the I-message, the parent is describing the behaviour which is of concern, and the consequences for the parent if the child continues the behaviour. In this case, the child becomes more aware of his/her behaviour, and is more likely to modify it with less resentment.

By definition, an I-message informs the child how the parent FEELS about the problem BEHAVIOUR, and tells the child the CONSEQUENCES of his/her behaviour for the parent. Using I-messages therefore, promotes honest recognition and expression of feelings in parent-child communication. Provide the following examples of parent owned problems for group members to practice the construction of I-messages.

Child breaks parent's favourite record.

Adolescent has the stereo too loud.

Child uses the telephone for long periods of time to ring friends.

I-messages may also indicate appreciation of the child's behaviour, for example

Parent says to a child who has cleaned up after making a snack, "I appreciated you putting things away after making your snack. It makes it easier for me to start getting tea ready."

7.   Homework.

Present exercises on the construction of I-messages and parent mediated problem solving practice.

Next session will continue to focus on I-messages and problem ownership. Natural and logical consequences will also be discussed.

Remind parents of the teacher training session to be held during the forthcoming week.

Homework: Session 6

OWNING PROBLEMS AND FRIENDLY COMMUNICATION

1. I-messages inform the child how the parent FEELS about the problem BEHAVIOUR, and tells the child the CONSEQUENCES of his/her behaviour for the parent.

    Construct I-messages for the following parent 'owned' problems, and write your responses next to each problem behaviour.

    1. Parent is on the telephone, and the child keeps interrupting.

        _____

        _____

    2. Child comes home late from sport's practice.

        _____

        _____

    3. Adolescent dresses in "scruffy" clothes for school social.

        _____

        _____

2. Use an appreciative I-message during the week. Record it for discussion next week.

    _____

    _____

3. Use STOP-THINK-DO with your child during the forthcoming week. Ensure the problem is one the child 'owns'.

    Write your own and your child's responses.

    _____

    _____

    _____

    _____

    _____

    _____

    _____

PARENT TRAINING PROGRAMME
SESSION 7: CONVEYING MESSAGES AND MORES,
AND APPLYING CONSEQUENCES

Aims of Session 7

- to practice I-messages which convey honest expression of feelings and respect.
- to practice STOP-THINK-DO problem solving method including strategy evaluation.
- to present natural and logical consequences as strategies for management of misbehaviour.
- to facilitate transfer of skills learned in session 7 of the child/adolescent programme, specifically skills to handle teasing and put downs, and to evaluate strategies and consequences in terms of the RIGHT (morally responsible) criterion.

Materials Required

- attendance chart
- video of "The Project" from the "What Should I Do?" series. If unavailable, a printed social problem situation is provided.
- video recorder and monitor
- blackboard and chalks, or paper and textas
- homework sheets for session 7
- refreshments

Procedure

Record attendance.

Confirm spouse/caregiver session to be held during the forthcoming week. Report to parents on the teacher training session held during the previous week to evaluate the utility of the STOP-THINK-DO approach in the school setting and the ability of teachers to mediate or facilitate in the social problem solving process with the children in the group. Discuss progress towards goal attainment from the teachers' perspective.

1. Review Discussion.

    Discuss with parents the application of the STOP-THINK-DO process in the home situation using homework examples. Highlight problem ownership, the use of open, reflective listening, and the questions used by the parents in the mediation process to encourage alternative solutions, the evaluation of consequences and the choice of an action. Discuss specific problems parents may be having with any of the steps involved.

    Check parents' understanding and use of I-messages in the homework exercises.

    Discuss examples of constructed I-messages which indicate how the parent FEELS about the child's BEHAVIOUR, and the CONSEQUENCES of the behaviour for the parent.

    Discuss also the use of appreciative I-messages. Examine the feelings of parents in expressing the messages, and the children's reactions to receiving them.

2. Information on the Child/Adolescent Programme.

    In session 7, the child programme focusses on problem solving strategy evaluation in terms of the RIGHT way criterion i.e. behaving in a responsible way when faced with moral dilemmas. The adolescent programme also focusses on solving problems involving moral questions (eg. drug taking, vandalism, stealing) when the possible consequences of behaviour need serious consideration. The handling of unfriendly negative responses (put downs, teasing) is further discussed. Refer to the relevant programme sessions for further details which may be utilized in the parent programme. Two parents volunteer to participate in the child group for shared problem solving practice.

3. I-messages and Angry I-messages.

Present the following vignette.

A parent has a book on loan from the local library. The elder child in the family has recently used it and left it lying around the house. A younger child has found it and scribbled over the cover. Whilst collecting books for return to the library, the parent notices the scribbling.

Ask parents to identify the parent's feelings, then the child's behaviour and the consequences of the behaviour for the parent in order to construct an I-message, for example,
"I get worried when library books are left lying around the house because the baby scribbles in them. The library staff could fine me for returning damaged books".

Then ask parents to construct a You-message. An example is
"You shouldn't leave library books around the place. You're just so careless".

Discuss the child's possible reactions to this You-message which might include the feedback of You-messages to the parent.
"You should have stopped the baby. It's your fault!"

Refer to session 7 of the adolescent programme for examples of popular parental and child put downs or You-messages. These negative statements provide a focus for discussion of the usual feelings and reactions which are aroused when You-messages are given.

Some I-messages may convey the same negative statements as the put down You-messages. For example, in the vignette considered, a response —
"I get angry when you leave books lying around the house. You know the baby always gets into things. I thought I could rely on you to look after things".

— conveys an angry I-message and denotes a disguised You-message and a put down by the parent.

Request examples from group members of angry I-messages. Ask parents to predict the child's possible reactions and therefore to discern what message is being communicated to the child (eg. blame, anger, hostility). Although the statement may begin, "I feel angry..", it eventually becomes a negative You-message. When anger is conveyed in an I-message, it denotes a disguised You-message or put down.

In constructing I-messages, it is necessary to identify and state the primary feeling. Behind anger, there is usually a more basic emotion eg. fear, worry, relief. For example, a parent allows an adolescent to go to the city with some friends, and the adolescent promises to be home before dark. However, the adolescent arrives home later than expected. The parent is very angry and critical of the adolescent for his/her irresponsible behaviour.

"You're so irresponsible! I hate it when you do this to me. Do you want to get hurt? You just do this to upset me".

These You-messages denote critical, angry, put downs. However, the parent's anger and criticism of the adolescent are subsequent to more basic feelings of fear, worry and eventual relief.

These feeling can be incorporated into an I-message which honestly reflects those feelings.

"I get so worried when you are out late. I am afraid something has happened to you".

The child's reaction to these honest I-messages is less likely to be a retaliatory You-message or parent put down (e.g. "You don't trust me").

4. I-messages and Moral Issues.

In relation to the parents' role in teaching their children the RIGHT way to behave in situations where there is a question about responsibility to conform to social mores, suggest that parents think carefully about the way they communicate these responsiblities to their children.

You-messages (eg. "You should be more responsible with public property"; "You can't have any feelings for us if you go out and steal"; "You shouldn't play with matches") often convey put downs of the child and will probably evoke similar responses, especially from adolescents who are under increasing pressure from another set of "You should..." rules from their peer group. Parents are advised to convey their feelings of disappointment, fear, worry, apprehension in I-messages which will not necessarily provoke negative reactions e.g. "I am really disappointed about what has happened;" "I am worried about the harmful effect of drugs and alcohol on young people". Such statements may be followed up with information which supports the parent's concern about the undesirable consequences of such behaviour. Since the child has not been "switched off" by a judgemental negative put down, he/she is more likely to continue to listen to the parent, and open communication and problem solving may be expected to follow.

The use of logical or natural consequences to be discussed shortly is well suited as a strategy for management of morally irresponsible behaviour. The logical consequences may not always be indicated by the parent; other members of society may also be involved.

5. Refreshments

Parents who participated in the children's session report on their observations. Allow time for discussion of relevant topics and practice of techniques as requested by parents.

6. Natural and Logical Consequences.

Refer to handout on Overview of Communication and Problem Solving Strategies. Natural and Logical Consequences (terms derived by Dreikurs & Soltz, 1972) refer to strategies for use for both child owned and parent owned problems. These strategies allow the children to realize the consequences of their behaviour and as a result, modify it. By using these strategies, parents indicate that they believe their children are capable of choosing solutions to problems. This promotes decision making and responsibility taking by their children.

The definitions of Natural and Logical Consequences are as follows:
"Natural Consequences represent the pressure of reality without any specific action by parents and are always effective... The natural flow of events occur without any interference from adults. Logical Consequences occur when parents structure events which logically follow the misdeed" (Dreikurs & Soltz, p77).

For example, if a child leaves his/her lunch at home, the natural consequences of this is for the child to feel hungry, and he/she is more likely to remember to take lunch the next day.

The following exemplifies the use of a logical consequence. The family dog is allowed in at night to sit in front of the fire. However, occasionally the child teases the dog and it gets excited, the result being that the child and the dog run through the house making considerable noise. The parent provides choices (i.e. logical consequences) to the child; either the dog goes outside when it becomes excited or, it stays outside all the time. If the child indicates that he wants the dog to remain inside at night, and at a later time teases the dog, the parent then follows through with the logical consequence of putting the dog outside at that time.

However, the parent indicates to the child that the dog may come in the following night. He tries not to annoy or excite the dog, thus learning self-control.

Thus with logical consequences the parent offers a choice of solutions to the child, follows through with the consequences if the child misbehaves but offers the child an opportunity at another time to behave appropriately in a similar situation.

Present the following examples of child and parent owned problems for discussion, and ask parents to decide upon ownership of the problem, and devise consequences for the behaviour.

— Adolescent leaves dirty clothes in his/her bedroom.
— Child's football is often kicked over the neighbour's fence.
— The neighbour is annoyed, and complains to the parent.

7.   Homework.

Exercises on I-messages, You-messages and Angry I-messages are set, together with examples of natural and logical consequences. Indicate that at the next session there will be a further inspection of natural and logical consequences using parents' examples, and a practice of concepts and techniques presented in previous sessions to "get it all together".

Homework: Session 7
CONVEYING MESSAGES AND MORES, AND APPLYING CONSEQUENCES

1. Devise natural and logical consequences for the following problems, and write your answers below:—

   1. Child/Adolescent forgets to do homework.

      _____

      _____

   2. Child/Adolescent leaves his/her belongings in the family room.

      _____

      _____

2. Record below an I-message, You-message, and an Angry I-message you used with your child during the week.

   1. I-message:

      _____

      _____

   2. You-message:

      _____

      _____

   3. Angry I-message:

      _____

      _____

3. Give an example of using an I-message to convey information to your child on a moral issue.

   _____

   _____

REMEMBER:

Continue to use open, reflective listening, and the STOP-THINK-DO problem solving approach.

PARENT TRAINING PROGRAMME
SESSION 7s: SPOUSE/CAREGIVER INVOLVEMENT

Aims of Session 7s

- to provide an opportunity for further discussion and practice of concepts and techniques presented in the previous spouse/caregiver meeting.
- to discuss problems in communication and management from the viewpoint of non-participating spouses/caregivers.
- to provide feedback on the progress of the children/adolescents in their group and at school.
- to broaden the base for extension of skills acquired by children and parents attending the weekly programme, by enlisting the support of significant others in the home environment.

Materials Required

- name tags
- video e.g. "The Lunch Money", from the "What Should I Do?" series or a printed social problem situation
- video recorder and monitor
- blackboard and chalks or paper and textas
- notes from child/adolescent group leaders and teachers regarding progress of the children in the programme
- refreshments

Procedure

Issue name tags.

Indicate aims of the session as outlined.

1. Information on the Child/Adolescent Social Skills Training Programme.
   Discuss the content of recent sessions of the children's group.
2. Goal Attainment

   Report on the progress towards attaining the goals set in the group for children whose parents are present.

   Obtain the viewpoint of spouses/caregivers regarding progress towards the achievement of goals for the home setting as identified in the previous meeting and to describe problems they have in relation to the reinforcement of skills and attitudes which would enhance goal achievement at home. Discuss also progress toward goal attainment in the school and peer related settings from the teachers' viewpoint.
3. Refreshments
4. Information on the Parent Training Programme

   Present the critical elements of recent sessions of the parent programme, including regular practice in the STOP-THINK-DO problem solving method and strategy evaluation according to the COOL/WEAK/AGGRO criteria. Describe strategies which involve FRIENDLY behaviour (showing consideration and respect for others). I-messages often fall into this category.

   Describe strategies which involve an evaluation of the RIGHT or morally responsible thing to do.

To demonstrate these principles and methods, show the video or present a problem situation for evaluation, following the steps outlined in the STOP-THINK-DO Problem Solving approach handout. Problem situations may also be proposed by parents for discussion and practice.

Include where applicable discussion of problems in terms of problem ownership, the use of I-messages, You-messages, and Angry I-messages.

Follow this with the construction of I-messages which convey honest feeling expression and promote positive communication between parent and child. Suggest the application of Natural and Logical consequences for managing behaviour. Refer to the video or practice examples for consequences of this nature which could follow the various proposed strategies and ways of behaving. Introduce the concept of the Family Get Together (refer to session 8 for details). All members of the family get together regularly to discuss family owned problems or family matters. This technique promotes consistency of approach and more active involvement by non-attending spouses/care-givers in skills training, transfer and maintenance for the child/adolescent in the programme.

Encourage parents to initiate the Family Get Together following session 8 using a positive 'problem' e.g. planning a family outing. Emphasize the importance of continual feedback between spouses/caregivers in each family regarding the concepts and techniques trained in the weekly sessions.

SESSION 8: CO-OPERATING AND GETTING IT TOGETHER

Aims of Session 8

- to further discuss the use of Natural and Logical Consequences as management strategies.
- to practice STOP-THINK-DO problem solving approach and strategy evaluation.
- to review parents' goals for themselves in the programme.
- to present the Family Get Together as a method for promoting consistency of approach, shared problem solving practice and active involvement of significant members of the family.
- to facilitate the transfer of skills learned by the child/adolescent in session 8 of their programme, specifically group problem solving and decision making skills the CO-OPERATIVE way.

Materials Required

- attendance chart
- goal sheets for parents
- homework sheets for session 8
- refreshments

Procedure

Record attendance.

Invite comments regarding the recent spouse/caregiver session.

1. Review Discussion

   Using the homework exercises as a base, review the use of natural and logical consequences for particular problem situations. Consider the concept of problem ownership in each situation, and the appropriateness of applying natural and logical consequences as solutions, providing the parent is able to follow through with the consequence if the child misbehaves.

   Alternatively suggest complementary techniques requiring open, reflective listening and the STOP-THINK-DO method with the evaluation of strategies and consequences, and final choice of action.

   Incorporate I-messages, You-messages and Angry I-messages where appropriate in the discussion of examples suggested by parents. Emphasize that when constructing an honest I-message, primary feelings need to be identified and incorporated in the message.

2. Information on Child/Adolescent Programme

   Discuss the content of session 8 of the child/adolescent programme. The focus is on group problem solving and decision making to serve the function of the group. Emphasis is placed on the evaluation of strategies for group problem solving using the CO-OPERATIVE way criterion. This suggests a balance between COOL behaviour and FRIENDLY behaviour, speaking up for one self and one's ideas while considering and respecting others in the group. Refer to session 8 of the child/adolescent programme for further details and practice exercises. Remind parents that the next session will be the final one for the children and will include a party which the children will plan as a co-operative exercise during the session.

Two parents join the child group to participate in shared problem solving practice using a group decision making and problem solving situation. This is the final session for such parental involvement.

3.   The STOP-THINK-DO Problem Solving Method Applied.

Using a parent example and the STOP-THINK-DO Problem Solving handout, revise the method including strategy evaluation. If shown previously in the group, refer to the video "The Project" as an example of group decision making and problem solving for the benefit of the group. Using this model if available, suggest that the parents discuss planning their own party to be held in week 10. Arrangements regarding what to bring and how to organize the session require co-operation between individuals. This process is required also for Family Get Togethers to be discussed later in the session.

4.   Natural and Logical Consequences

Using parent examples of problem situations, devise natural and logical consequences for the children's behaviour. Consider the development and formulation of choices for the children to promote their decision making and responsibility taking skills.

Emphasize that consequences need to be ones parents can act upon. Moreover, after parents follow through with logical consequences, an opportunity for the children to behave appropriately should be offered.

At times, parent expectations regarding the child's behaviour and the parent's own behaviour are divergent. eg. the parent who expects the child to tidy up his/her belongings left in the family room, but leaves the parent's own possessions strewn around the house. When issuing logical consequences for, or allowing natural consequences to follow their children's behaviour, parents need to be aware of the examples they set for this behaviour.

5.   Refreshments

Parents report on their observations in the child group session. Allow time for discussion of topics suggested by parents.

6.   Parent Goals

In a supportive and constructive manner, discuss parents' goals as identified in earlier sessions. Evaluate the attainment of these goals with feedback given by group members. Focus on the skills acquired and those requiring further practice.

7.   Family Get Together

Considering problem ownership leads to decisions about which strategies to utilize to solve the problem at hand. However, there are occasions when both parent and child own or share the problem, for example going on a family outing in terms of where to go, and what to do. Also although parents may have tried various strategies, there may be some problems which recur, e.g. distribution of jobs.

A method to deal with shared and recurring problems effectively and positively in terms of family relationships is to hold a regular Family Get Together to discuss issues of concern and to plan family activities or solve recurring problems. This meeting of all family members is scheduled for a set time on a regular basis and is initially chaired by a parent to model effective and appropriate communication skills such as open, reflective listening, I-messages, and STOP-THINK-DO to facilitate discussion. This assists the family group to make decisions regarding appropriate solutions to situations involving family members (problem or otherwise).

Consider the following roleplay of a Family Get Together. Enlist group members as the participants. Kathy is 9 years, Tom 11 years, and Sarah 14.

159

Father:	"Okay, it's Mum's turn to be leader this week".
Mother:	"Well let's just see how we went with our decisions from last time before we look at the things that are worrying us now".
Tom:	"Aw do we have to do this? I'm sick of it".
Mother:	"You feel bored Tom when we review what we discussed last time".
Tom:	"Yeh, why can't we just get on with it so I can go and watch T.V.?"
Mother:	"You'd rather watch T.V. than spend time going over what we did to solve problems".
Tom:	"It's just that my favourite programme is on".
Mother:	"Well Tom if you wish to go and watch T.V. you can, but remember that whatever we decide upon, goes until our next Family Get Together".
Tom:	"Oh that's not fair".
Mother:	"Perhaps you can talk about the time of the Family Get Together later. Let's get going. Last time we decided to plan to go out together. We decided that Tom, Kathy, and Dad would go to the Lego Exhibition, Sarah and I would go to the Museum because of Sarah's project, and we would meet afterwards, get take aways and have it at the city park. What did you all think of our family outing?"
Tom:	"The Lego was great especially the cars and aeroplanes too." (Makes noise of car and demonstrates aeroplane).
Sarah:	"Oh stop it Tom. Anyway it helped me get my project done".
Mother:	"Good, so you both enjoyed yourselves. What about you Kathy?"
Kathy (dejectedly):	"It was alright I suppose. I wish someone would show lots of Barbie dolls instead of Lego".
Father:	"You were disappointed Kathy because you didn't see your favourite things".
Kathy:	"Yeh".
Father:	"Perhaps you might want to talk about doing some favourite things when we list our ideas".
Kathy:	"Great. I'd like to go horse-riding".
Tom:	"I want to go and watch the cars race, and go to the BMX track with Dad, and go and watch the cricket".
Mother:	"Okay, okay; you've got lots of ideas. Dad, what did you think about our family outing?"
Father:	"Well I enjoyed going to the Lego with Kathy and Tom. I hadn't realized all the designs that could be made with Lego".
Mother:	"That's the same with me. I hadn't been to the Museum for years. It was a good chance to look at some recent discoveries. I thought it was great to meet up afterwards and have lunch without having to worry about cooking and cleaning up. Actually that's one problem I have that I could list in a moment".
Mother:	"Shall we go onto our problem list then? Let's see Tom, what were you worried about?' Oh yes, the time of the meeting".

The chairperson invites all the family members to present and define their problems in turn. They have an opportunity to state how they feel about the problem, what they want to happen and along with other family members to offer solutions for the problem. The family then reaches a consensus on the most appropriate solution to try. The chairperson suggests a trial period to put the strategy into practice with a review at the next Family Get Together. Indicate to parents that the chairperson's role may be rotated once the Family Get Together is established.

Encourage group members to indicate the use by the chairperson in the roleplay of concepts and techniques learned in previous sessions.

These include reflective listening, logical consequences, problem ownership and encouragement. In terms of the concepts stressed in the child/adolescent programme, the efficacy of the Family Get Together depends on CO-OPERATIVE behaviour between family members i.e. COOL and FRIENDLY behaviour requiring the individual members to speak up for themselves yet show consideration, fairness and respect for others.

8. Homework

To utilize the concepts and techniques learned to organize and conduct a Family Get Together this week.

Next session will review these concepts and techniques.

Homework: Session 8
CO-OPERATING AND GETTING IT TOGETHER

1. Try a Family Get Together during the week and report on it.

_____

_____

_____

_____

_____

_____

_____

_____

2. During the meeting, utilize concepts of open, reflective listening, STOP-THINK-DO problem solving approach, I-messages, natural and logical consequences, problem ownership COOL, FRIENDLY and CO-OPERATIVE ways of behaving.

    Bring examples of these to the next group session for discussion.

_____

_____

_____

_____

_____

_____

_____

_____

SESSION 9: PRACTICING SKILLS AND EVALUATING PROGRESS

Aims of Session 9

- to practice concepts and techniques presented in the parent programme including critical components of the child/adolescent social skills training programme.
- to evaluate progress, skill acquisition and goal attainment for parents and their children from the parents' viewpoint.

Materials Required

- attendance chart
- blackboard and chalks, paper and textas
- Parent Forms: POST GROUP (Appendix 6) and pens
- refreshments

Procedure

Record attendance.

1. Review Discussion

   Parents are encouraged to discuss each family's Get Together, outlining the techniques used and the problems encountered with reference to the homework exercise. Discuss parents' reactions and concerns, and also children's reactions to the meeting. Suggest parents schedule further meetings to review decisions made in the initial meeting and to allow an opportunity to discuss current problem situations, especially those involving shared problem ownership or recurring misbehaviours.

2. Information on Child/Adolescent Programme

   Session 9 in the child/adolescent programme focusses on the evaluation of goals achieved in the group with feedback between group peers. Additionally saying goodbye is presented as an interpersonal problem to solve.

   The final party is presented as a co-operative planning and decision making exercise for the group as a whole.

3. Review of Concepts and Techniques

   Discuss topics raised by parents with particular reference to the utilization and practical application of concepts and techniques presented in the programme.

   Encourage parents to raise current problem issues regarding the implementation of the techniques in the home environment.

   Discuss the consistency of approach between spouses/caregivers in the same family and the extent of involvement of the non-participating partner in the reinforcement of acquired skills in the home.

4. Refreshments

5. Practice of Concepts and Techniques.

   Provide a list of problem situations for parents to apply concepts and techniques regarding

   — ownership of the problem
   — strategies to use

— examples of actions or statements they would do or say

The list may include:—

> 6 year old Robert refuses to go to bed at the scheduled time.
>
> 10 year old Susan cleans her bedroom without reminders.
>
> Karen who is 8 years of age leaves her bicycle on the driveway.
>
> The Smith children aged 10 years and 14 years fight about T.V. programmes whilst their father who is in the same room tries to read the newspaper.
>
> At the last Family Get Together, 8 year old Jim volunteered to feed the animals. However he has failed on 3 successive days to do this job.
>
> Craig aged 13 years arrives home late from school, and is angry because his bus pass has been stolen.
>
> The school principal telephones to say that 15 year old Amanda was caught with a bottle of rum at the school social.
>
> Your son Thomas who is 12 years old blames his friend Tim who is also 12 for making him steal some lollies from a shop.
>
> 9 year olds Lisa and Paula who have been friends for a long time, have had an argument and will not speak to each other.

6. Parent Forms: POST GROUP completed by parents.

    Indicate that the children will complete similar forms. Remind parents of school visits to be arranged in the forthcoming week to obtain teacher post group evaluations and also ratings of school peer acceptance (7 — 12 year olds).

    The information obtained from post group evaluations from children (self), parents, teachers and peers will be discussed in the next session.

7. Remind parents of commitments made for the party for parents next session.

8. Leaders' Meeting

    Leaders from parent and child/adolescent groups meet to evaluate post group progress in terms of skills acquired and goals achieved for children and parents attending the programme.

PARENT TRAINING PROGRAMME
SESSION 10: FEEDBACK

Aims of Session 10

- to provide feedback to parents regarding skill acquisition and goal achievement for their children in the group and school environments.

- to obtain feedback from parents regarding skill acquisition and goal achievement in the home related environment.

- to make further recommendations for follow-up.

- to arrange a 3 month review evaluation of the maintenance and generalization of positive outcomes from the programme.

Materials Required

- attendance chart
- goal sheets for children, parents and teachers
- refreshments, party supplies

Procedure

Record attendance.

If a fee has been charged for programme involvement, part may be reimbursed for regular maintained attendance.

1. Party

    Parents organize catering. Parents and leaders may help themselves during the feedback session. Leaders from both parent and child/adolescent groups meet with parents for feedback.

2. Parent Feedback

    Parents describe the children's progress over the term from the perspective of the home. Referring to goal sheets completed in early sessions and to responses on the parent post group evaluation forms completed last session, check goal attainment and skill acquisition for children and parents from the parents' viewpoint.

3. Child/Adolescent Group Leader Feedback

    Leaders from child/adolescent group report on the children's progress in terms of their understanding and application of essential concepts and techniques. Indicate the level of active involvement and positive participation in the group programme by each member. Highlight positive behaviours and attributes. Describe the development of peer relationships in the group. Comment on personal and interpersonal goal attainment in the group, referring to goal sheets and also self report forms completed last session by the children.

    Refer also to the goals set by group peers who provided support and encouragement for social skills acquisition and social goal direction.

4. Teacher Feedback

    Summarize the teachers' comments and ratings of the progress made by the child in terms of social skill acquisition and peer acceptance as viewed by the teachers in the school context. Provide examples of positive behaviours noted by the teachers.

165

5. School Peer Feedback (7 — 12 year group)

Evaluate peer acceptance of each child in the group in terms of the likability of the child and acceptability as a playmate or friend as reflected in the sociometric ratings obtained from school peers.

6. Summary and Recommendations

Discuss the compatibility and consistency of the reports from the various significant perspectives included in the programme.

Note current concerns expressed by the various raters regarding persistent social problems, skills deficits or poor social motivation.

Make recommendations for further remediation e.g. involvement in community groups, encouraging age mates to visit the home, encouraging the practice of STOP by impulsive children and DO by inhibited children.

Booster social skills training sessions may also be offered.

Indicate that parents, teachers and referring persons will receive written summaries of progress and further recommendations.

7. Review Session

A date and time is set for Review in 3 months time.

Encourage attendance at the review session in order to evaluate the maintenance and transfer of positive outcomes from the training programme for children and parents. School visits will be arranged prior to the Review to obtain teacher and school peer ratings (7 — 12 year old group) to indicate maintenance of goals in the school situation and peer related contexts. This information will be fedback to parents at the Review session.

Parents are encouraged to maintain contact with group leaders over the review period if required.

PARENT TRAINING PROGRAMME
REVIEW: MAINTENANCE AND GENERALIZATION

Aims of Review Session

- to renew acquaintances.
- to evaluate maintenance of parents' goals, and report on application of techniques learned in the parent training programme.
- to evaluate the current social behaviour and attitudes of the children who attended the programme.
- to provide feedback to parents regarding progress from the viewpoints of teachers, school peers and the children themselves.
- to make further recommendations for management and goal attainment.

Materials Required

- goal achievement charts for parents and children completed in final session of each group
- refreshments
- Parent Forms: REVIEW (Appendix 7) and pens

Procedure

1. Renew acquaintances

   Discuss contacts maintained between parents and/or children over the past 3 months.

2. Review Parent Goals

   Present parents' goals identified for themselves at the commencement of the group, and attained by the completion of the group programme. Ask parents to indicate the extent to which their goals have been maintained.

   Discuss the need to re-establish goals if they have not been maintained and/or define new goals for themselves.

3. Skill Maintenance

   Evaluate the utility of the concepts and techniques learned in the parent training programme. Discuss specific problems which parents may be experiencing with the application of these techniques.

   Review the critical elements of reflective listening, appropriate use of attending behaviour, problem ownership, I-messages, natural and logical consequences, the Family Get Together, the STOP-THINK-DO approach to social problem solving and the parent's mediating, facilitating role in the development of the child's own problem solving and behavioural skills.

   Critical elements of the child/adolescent programme are also reviewed including feeling recognition, social problem solving, strategy evaluation in terms of COOL/WEAK/AGGRO, FRIENDLY, RIGHT and CO-OPERATIVE criteria, behavioural skills development and social motivational orientation.

4. Parent Forms: REVIEW completed by parents.

5. Refreshments.

6. Feedback

   Leaders from child/adolescent group join parent review session to discuss progress in terms of the reports obtained from teachers, school peers (7 — 12 year old groups) and

167

the children themselves in their Review ratings of social behaviours, skills deficits and peer acceptance. Comment on the consistency and compatibility of reports from various viewpoints and also on the maintenance and generalization of positive outcomes of the intervention programme.

Make recommendations for future management including further goal formulation and skills acquisition.

Encourage parents to maintain contact with group leaders if required.

Chapter 6
Teacher
Training Programme

Chapter 6:
Teacher Training Programme

OUTLINE

Pre Group: Teacher involvement in assessment and planning.

Session 1: Solving social problems in the school with STOP-THINK-DO.

Session 2: Evaluation of STOP-THINK-DO approach in the school setting.

Post Group: Teacher involvement in evaluation.

Review: Maintenance and generalization.

TEACHER TRAINING PROGRAMME
PRE GROUP: TEACHER INVOLVEMENT IN ASSESSMENT
AND PROGRAMME PLANNING

Aims of Pre Group Involvement
- to introduce the teachers of the children/adolescents participating in the social skills training programme to the aims and methods of the programme.
- to obtain information regarding the peer relationships and social problems of the children referred, as seen by the teacher in the school situation.
- to enlist the support of teachers and schools in reinforcing skills learned in the group.
- to determine the social goal orientation of each teacher specifically in relation to their expectations for the child/adolescent attending the group.
- to determine school peer acceptance prior to intervention.

Materials Required
- General Information Leaflets (Appendix 8)
- Teacher Report Forms: PRE GROUP (Appendix 9)
- Peer Rating Forms (PRE) 7 — 12 year group (Appendix 16)
  The Peer rating forms are not designed for use with children attending secondary school, i.e. above the age of 12 years.

Procedure

Leaders from the child/adolescent group share the responsibility for teacher contact for the children in the group whose parents have given permission for teacher involvement. For children in the 7 — 12 year group, class teachers are involved. For children at secondary school, the teachers who have most contact with the children or the care group teachers who can relate information to and from all teachers are the most suitable persons to contact.

Following session 1, leaders telephone teachers to arrange school visits to

1. Discuss the current social and peer relationship problems of children in the group as seen by teachers in the school situation.

2. Identify the goals teachers would like the children to achieve by attending the social skills training group.

3. Ask teachers to complete Teacher Forms: PRE GROUP which will provide a more formal record of the information obtained in the discussion.

4. Provide General Information Leaflets regarding the social skills training programme and introduce the STOP-THINK-DO method of social problem solving.

5. Invite the teachers to Teacher Training Sessions in weeks 3 and 6 of the group. Provide date, time and location of meetings. Suggest that the sessions will be of 2 hours duration.

6. Peer Rating Forms (for 7 — 12 year group).

   At each school visit, choose four names at random from the teacher's roll book of children of the same sex as the child in the group.

   Record these names plus the target child in random order on the peer rating form. The form may then be photocopied to provide sufficient sheets for all children of the same sex as the target child in the class. To reduce time, the teacher may provide the names at the telephone contact so that sheets may be prepared beforehand. Teachers need to be urged to give a random selection (say, every fourth child on the roll for same — sex children).

In the classroom, the target child is not identified specifically by the leader, other than a greeting if initiated by the child. The children are asked to sit on their own. The forms are handed to the classmates of the same sex as the target child (including the target child) with the following instructions adjusted to suit the age of the children:—

"We are here today to find out more about how children get on with each other.

On this form are some names of children in your class. Your name might be there.

We want to have your own ideas, so you don't need to let anyone else see your form.

Look at the first question.

How much do you play with......?

Now, look at the first name on the list. Tick whether you play with that person not at all, a little bit, quite a lot or heaps.

Then, look at the next name on the list and tick the box suitable for them and so on for all the children on the list."

Older children grasp the requirements of the task easily while younger children may need someone to monitor their understanding of the task.

When the children have completed the first question, say

"Look at the second question.

How much do you like .....?

Now look at the first name on the list. Tick whether you like that person not at all, a little bit and so on.

Make sure you tick one box for each of the children on the list.

Now, do the same for the third question.

Is .... your friend?"

Collect the forms.

7. Encourage the teachers to maintain contact with group leaders, and to attend the Teacher Training Sessions in weeks 3 and 6 where the basic principles and methods of the programme will be explained in depth.

TEACHER TRAINING PROGRAMME.
SESSION 1: SOLVING SOCIAL PROBLEMS IN THE SCHOOL WITH STOP-THINK-DO.

Aims of Session 1

- to formally instruct the teachers of the children/adolescents in the social skills training programme in the STOP-THINK-DO approach to social problem solving.
- to encourage teachers to reinforce the children for using this method in the classroom, playground and other school related environments.
- to encourage the general application by teachers of this common sense method to the broader class and school population.
- to clarify the concerns of teachers regarding the social problems of the children referred to the programme and the goals the teachers hope they achieve by attendance.

Materials Required

- large sheets of paper, textas
- STOP-THINK-DO posters (Appendix 18)
- STOP-THINK-DO Handout for Teachers (Appendix 25 for 7 — 12 year groups: 26 for adolescent groups)
- personal and group goal sheets for each child (from sessions 1 and 3) or adolescent (sessions 1 and 2)
- notes from session 3 recording the expectations of the children/adolescents about the goals their teachers may identify
- notes from parent group regarding parents' goals for the children
- video recorder and monitor
- video from the "What Should I Do ?" series (Additional Resource Materials)
- refreshments

Procedure

1. Introduction.

   Introduce leaders and invite introductions from teachers. Invite comments from teachers regarding the initial school visits, or the General Information Leaflets they received. Explain that the purpose of this session is to provide training for teachers in the social cognitive problem solving method which is central to the social skills training programme running concurrently for children/adolescents and their parents.

2. STOP-THINK-DO Video.

   Show one of the videos presented to the children. Refer to the STOP-THINK-DO posters and distribute the handout for teachers. Trace the step by step sequence as the children/adolescents/parents are taught, in order to solve the particular problem presented in the video. Encourage teachers to generate a number of alternative solutions and evaluate possible consequences of these alternatives.

3. Relevance of STOP-THINK-DO.

   Most people with poor relationships and poor social skills have difficulties somewhere along the STOP-THINK-DO sequence. For instance, acting out children often experience peer rejection because they do not STOP and THINK before they act — they just react spontaneously to their feelings or the actions of others. Also, what they DO and how they DO it often lacks skill and maturity. Shy children, although not necessarily rejected, may experience peer neglect because they STOP and hesitate but are unable to THINK of more effective ways of relating or lack the skills to DO them.

4. Application

Discuss the social difficulties of each child/adolescent with their teacher in terms of the child's ability to cope with each stage in the STOP-THINK-DO process. Ask each teacher to give examples of social situations which the child has difficulty handling. From these determine the stage in the STOP-THINK-DO sequence which is most problematic for the child. It may be useful to distinguish social problems involving peers from those including adults.

(a) Example for Children aged 7 — 12 years.

Take an example of a social problem situation described by a teacher which involves the child and his/her peers. Suggest the following approach by the teacher when a similar situation is observed in the future.

The teacher approaches the children concerned and says,

"Let's stop a minute".

"What is the problem here?".

If the child(ren) does not respond to verbal cues, attract their attention by using a hand clap or turn the child(ren) to face the traffic light motto on the wall. Using terms with which the teacher feels comfortable, he/she continues,

"How would you feel if that happened to you?" or

"How do you both feel about what happened?"

"What do you want to happen?"

Encourage children to look at each other to recognize feelings and goals, and to listen to what the other is saying. In the current school curriculum, there is a growing component concerned with feeling recognition and appropriate ways of feeling expression. Teachers may use the terminology included in the curriculum.

It is important to emphasize that teachers are not taking the role of referee or judge, but rather as a mediator in the process of feeling and goal identification, and problem solving.

The teacher encourages each child to THINK about a possible solution to the social problem.

"What can you do to solve the problem?"

In the initial stages, the teacher offers suggestions if children are reluctant, or elicits suggestions from other children.

Following each person's suggestion, encourage consequential thinking by asking,

"What might happen if you did that?"

"And how would you feel if that happened?"

When a solution has been found which has acceptable consequences for both parties, urge action.

"You seem to agree on that, so go ahead and DO it!"

Check with the children later whether the solution worked so that they both felt okay. If it did, reinforce their good thinking.

If the problem has arisen again or was not resolved, suggest

"If that way didn't work this time, think of another solution to try. There is always an answer if you STOP and THINK". If the child is shy and reluctant to put solutions into action, it is useful for another child to model the chosen solution before urging the hesitant child. The action may also be broken down into smaller steps, with the teacher or other child making the first move. They then assist the reluctant child to complete the action, decreasing the amount of assistance as more practice is gained.

(b)   Example for Young Adolescents.

Adolescents may resent such obvious intrusion into their social problems with peers. Many secondary school teachers also feel that adolescents need to accept responsibility for their own problems and prefer to opt out of conflicts involving students. Adolescents who are experiencing social problems however, benefit from guidance by teachers who are sensitive to the needs of the child and the situation, and who are trained in an effective social problem solving technique.

Take an example of a social problem situation described by a teacher which involves the adolescent and his/her peers.

Suggest the following approach which contains the elements of STOP-THINK-DO, but in a less structured format. The teacher approaches those concerned and says,

"I noticed that you seem to be having a problem".

"I can see you are upset (angry, miserable etc)".

This initial step is one of feeling reflection, a component of STOP. Often this approach is better received when the people are approached individually following the incident, away from peer inspection. The teacher, having gained the attention of the child(ren) continues,

"Can you both think of ways of working the problem out?" or,

"Have you thought about what you can do about it?" if approached individually.

In the initial stages, the teacher offers suggestions if the child is reluctant.

"What could happen if you did that?" or,

"What might that lead to?"

"How would you feel about that?" or,

"Is that what you want?"

Adolescents often will not volunteer information to teachers about what they could or will do, and may not participate actively in the above process, at least initially. The children involved in the social skills training programme will be accustomed to this approach in the group and at home, and are likely to be more receptive in the school situation provided the approach is applied sensitively by teachers. Whether or not the child actively participates in the process outlined, the teacher concludes,

"There is always an answer if you THINK about it".

"I would be interested to hear what you DO to work it out".

After a while, check with those concerned. Reinforce good thinking if the problem is resolved or more thinking if it recurs. By showing sensitivity and guidance yet not intrusiveness into the adolescent's peer problems, the teacher is acting, not so much as a **mediator** as with younger children, but as a **facilitator** for social problem solving.

174

School counsellors generally receive training in techniques such as problem solving and conflict resolution, and may be good local resource persons for the teachers involved in the programme to improve their skills in these areas. Additionally, school counsellors may be called in to facilitate the problem solving process for the target child/adolescent in particular situations.

5. Modelling.

Suggest to the teachers the benefits of utilizing this "thinking" approach themselves in the many different social problem situations which arise in the classroom and yard. The teachers will serve as a significant model for the children and adolescents in the training programme, as well as their peers at school.

6. Positive Feedback.

Stress the importance of teachers recognizing the attempts of the children/adolescents at problem solving practice in the school setting, especially by using social reinforcement (praise, positive comments). For younger children, more tangible rewards such as stickers or fun activities may be useful.

7. A Step towards Primary Prevention.

Teachers usually find difficulty in "singling out" children for special treatment (e.g. with rewards for good thinking). In addition, teachers often express that they have a number of children with social problems of varying degrees in their class.

The approach outlined, however, is well adapted to the entire classroom and schoolyard situation and to the myriad of social relations and interactions within it.

Urge teachers to generalize their training in the STOP-THINK-DO method into the broader school environment, including direct instruction in the classroom. In primary school classes, children may make posters or badges to display on walls or books to remind them of the essential steps in the process. The target child need not be identified as attending a special programme if they are reluctant for this to be known.

However, some children enjoy relating their group experiences to their classmates. The teacher in this case may use the child's homework as a class exercise and basis for class discussion.

Other staff in the school may also be interested in extending the approach into their classrooms. School counsellors may be involved in the generalization process.

The social problem solving method aims to reduce conflict between classmates and teachers/pupils through the development of prosocial thinking habits and the prevention of social skills deficits in the problem solving area.

8. Break.

Refreshments and informal conversation.

9. Teacher Goals.

Clarify the expectations of teachers for the children/adolescents attending the group. Specifically identify the goals they hope the children will achieve. Record the responses for comparison with the children's goals for themselves, the parents' goals for their children and the group goals identified by their peers in the social skills training group. Discuss the commonalities, discrepancies and compatibilities of the goals identified from the different perspectives. The teachers may also be interested in what the children expected them to say about their social problems.

10. Goal Achievement Planning.

For each child/adolescent in the group, choose 2 prosocial goals identified by the teacher which are also compatible with the child's goal orientation. Discuss a plan of action for achieving these goals in the school setting. The plan will involve mediation/facilitation by the teacher using STOP-THINK-DO in social situations where the child/adolescent can practice skills compatible with these goals.

(a) Example for children 7 — 12 years.

Consider 10 year old Jeffrey referred to the social skills training programme for his immature and aggressive behaviour.

Compatible goals for group attendance:

Jeffrey — "make more friends".

Mother — "learn to act his age and not be so rough".

Teacher — "learn to join in group activities rather than aggravate children".

Plan of action for teacher in school situation:

— call STOP in group situations where Jeffrey is behaving immaturely or aggressively with other children and ask the children for feedback on the problem and their feelings about it.

— encourage Jeffrey and the other children to THINK about alternative ways of behaving in view of his desire to make more friends, and to DO what will have the result he most values, urging positive feedback from the other children.

— reinforce his efforts and suggest he stop and think again if the problem recurs.

— reinforce other children behaving appropriately as models for Jeffrey.

(b) Example for young adolescents.

Consider 14 year old Maryanne referred to the social skills training programme for her extreme shyness and social withdrawal. Compatible goals for group attendance:

Maryanne — "to learn to speak up for myself".

Parents — "to come out of her shell".

Teacher — "to learn to initiate conversation".

Plan of action for teacher in school situation:

— take Maryanne aside in social situations where she is withdrawing or not participating and reflect back her apparent discomfort or sadness (soft STOP).

— encourage her to THINK about the alternative things she could do in view of her wish to be able to speak up in company, and encourage her to think about the likely effects of each way.

— urge her to try to DO what might bring the results she wants. If she is reluctant to make any moves, suggest a small step to begin with, and more steps next time.

— reinforce Maryanne's efforts and elicit positive feedback from peers.

In relation to planning for goal achievement, discuss with teachers the suggestions provided by adolescents in session 2 about various ways in which teachers can help them achieve their goals.

11. Follow-up Contact.

Invite teachers to maintain contact with group leaders throughout the term. Remind them of the details of the follow-up teacher training session in week 6. Encourage a commitment to attend. Indicate that the STOP-THINK-DO method will be evaluated in terms of its viability in the school setting. Urge them to remember particular examples where they assisted the child to use the method to be discussed at the next teacher session.

SESSION 2: EVALUATION OF STOP-THINK-DO APPROACH
IN THE SCHOOL SETTING.

Aims of Session 2

- to evaluate the utility of the STOP-THINK-DO method for solving social problems in the school setting.
- to obtain feedback from teachers regarding the progress of children/adolescents in the group towards goal achievement in the school setting.
- to provide feedback to teachers regarding the progress of the children/adolescents towards goal achievement in the social skills group and home setting.
- to discuss the COOL/WEAK/AGGRO response styles and their effectiveness in solving social problems.

Materials Required

- paper, textas, pens
- STOP-THINK-DO posters
- COOL/WEAK/AGGRO poster (Appendix 19)
- COOL/WEAK/AGGRO Handouts (Appendix 24)
- forms for Evaluation of STOP-THINK-DO Approach in the School Setting (Appendix 27)
- goal sheets from previous teacher training session fixed on walls
- friendliness sheets from session 6 of child/adolescent group
- refreshments

Procedure

1. Renew acquaintances.
2. Evaluation of STOP-THINK-DO.

   Distribute forms to be completed by teachers evaluating the utility of the STOP-THINK-DO approach to social problem solving in relation to the target children/adolescents and classmates in the school setting.

   Collect completed forms.
3. Review of Method.

   Select examples from question 2 of the above form which describe social situations where the teacher used the method to assist a child in problem solving. Trace the steps in the process with input from the teacher involved in each example.

   Invite alternative solutions or methods of management from other teachers.
4. Difficulties with Application.

   Discuss teacher responses to question 3 on the form regarding the difficulties they have encountered using the method in the school setting. Difficulties may include

   —time constraints in the initial stages of learning the method.

   —undermining by other staff or children.

   —misinterpretation of this "talking out" method as a sign of weakness.

—involuntary or passive participation by child/adolescent.

—teacher's lack of confidence or patience in the learning stages.

Invite and offer suggestions to help overcome such difficulties.

5. Generalization of Method.

    Discuss responses to question 6 on the form regarding ways teachers have extended the method to their class in general.

    Discuss also problems encountered in doing so.

6. Goal Achievement.

    Refer to goal sheets completed by teachers last training session.

    Ask each teacher to evaluate progress towards goal achievement. Record their responses

    Review the plan of action outlined for each teacher and child/adolescent. Discuss the viability of these plans and make modifications if necessary.

    Provide feedback to the teachers regarding progress towards goal achievement in the group and in the home situation as reported by parents.

    Display the friendliness sheets for the children/adolescents as completed by their peers in the social skills group. Discuss the compatibility of group goals towards more friendly behaviour with teacher perceptions of the child's friendliness in school peer interactions.

7. Break (10 mins).

8. COOL/WEAK/AGGRO Response Styles.

    Distribute handout on COOL/WEAK/AGGRO response styles. This way of describing behaviour is useful in the THINK stage of STOP-THINK-DO when alternative solutions are proposed for evaluation.

    Take a social problem situation from question 2 on the Evaluation of STOP-THINK-DO form which could be solved by politely assertive behaviour eg. a person wants to join in an activity in which others are already involved. They virtually ignore the person when he/she asks to be included. Roleplay the situation with one leader taking the role of the person trying to join in.

    AGGRO. The leader first roleplays an aggressive solution eg. pushes way into group and makes demands. The other leader calls "STOP" and asks the teachers to discuss the technique used in terms of facial expression, body gesture, voice tone and feelings conveyed.

    Refer to handout. A person who is behaving in an AGGRO way:—

    shouts, yells.
    speaks rudely, abuses, teases, puts down.
    blames others.
    looks mad.
    stands close and threatens.
    pushes, hits, kicks.
    feels angry, annoyed, out of control.

    Discuss also the likely consequences of such behaviour. Evaluate the effectiveness of this method for solving the person's problem of wanting to join in the activity.

    How would the people involved feel afterwards?

    WEAK. The leader then roleplays a passive response. eg. stands to the side of the group and sulks. The other leader calls "STOP" and discusses the technique used in terms of

179

facial expressions, body gestures, voice tone and feelings conveyed. A person who is behaving in a WEAK way:—

>talks softly, mumbles.
>cries or sulks when faced with a problem.
>looks down at the floor.
>stands far away, hunched over.
>feels shy, embarrassed, nervous, useless, unhappy.

Discuss the possible consequences of such behaviour and evaluate the effectiveness of this method for solving the problem.

How would those involved feel afterwards?

COOL. Leader then roleplays a reasonably assertive response — approaching someone and asking firmly and positively.

Other leader again leads the discussion about this technique.

A person who is behaving in a COOL way:—

>speaks firmly but friendly.
>stands up for self politely.
>smiles or looks calm.
>stands tall.
>looks other person in the eyes.
>feels happy, confident, in control, okay about self.

Discuss the likely consequences of COOL behaviour and evaluate its effectiveness for solving the problem at hand.

How would the people involved feel afterwards?

Ask each teacher to describe the way the child or children behaved in the situation they depicted in question 2 according to the COOL/WEAK/AGGRO criteria.

Compare the consequences of COOL, WEAK and AGGRO response styles and how those involved feel afterwards.

Emphasize that the COOL way generally has the most acceptable consequences, and is, therefore often the solution to encourage children to choose and try first.

9. COOL/WEAK/AGGRO Applied.

Explain to teachers that these descriptive terms are used in the child/adolescent and parent programmes as an abbreviated means of conceptualizing strategies and making implications about likely consequences. Teachers may find it useful to apply these terms to different solutions while mediating or facilitating in the STOP-THINK-DO process in the school setting.

Most social behaviour may be described in these terms and children will learn to make quick implications about likely consequences and their relative desirability.

10. Teacher Commitment.

Refer to the last question on the form evaluating STOP-THINK-DO, regarding the teachers' commitment to continue applying the method with the target children and classmates.

Discuss the concerns of those teachers who reply negatively or are unsure.

11. Follow-Up.

Invite teachers to maintain contact with group leaders.

Remind them of the follow-up school visit following session 9 of the child/adolescent group.

TEACHER TRAINING PROGRAMME
POST GROUP: TEACHER INVOLVEMENT IN EVALUATION

Aims of Post Group Involvement

- to provide and obtain feedback regarding the progress of the children/adolescents in the group and at school.
- to evaluate goal achievement from the teachers' perspective.
- to make and obtain recommendations for follow–up.
- to determine school peer acceptance following intervention.

Materials Required

- teachers' goal sheets completed in teacher training sessions
- Teacher Forms: POST GROUP (Appendix 10)
- Peer Rating Forms (POST) for 7 — 12 year group (Appendix 16)

Procedure

Following session 9, leaders take responsibility to telephone the same teachers as previously to arrange school visits to

1. Provide feedback to teachers about the progress of the children/adolescents in the group and at home.
2. Obtain feedback from teachers regarding progress in the school setting and to evaluate the achievement of goals from the teachers' perspective.
3. Ask teachers to complete Teacher Forms: POST GROUP.
4. Make and obtain further recommendations regarding management and goal direction. Encourage teachers to continue utilizing the principles of the social skills training programme to ensure the maintenance of goals and the attainment of new ones.
5. Discuss the utility of the STOP-THINK-DO approach applied to the classroom and school yard generally.
6. Offer suggestions about problems teachers have encountered when applying the method to target children or other pupils.
7. Advise teachers of a review in three months where they will be contacted for a progress report. Invite them to maintain contact.
8. Advise teachers that they will receive a written Social Skills Programme Evaluation Report following the completion of both child/adolescent and parent programmes (Appendix 15).
9. Peer Rating Forms completed as discussed in Pre Group Teacher Involvement.

TEACHER TRAINING PROGRAMME
REVIEW:MAINTENANCE AND GENERALIZATION

Aims of Teacher Involvement at Review

- to obtain feedback regarding progress in the school setting of children/adolescents who attended the Social Skills training group three (3) months previously.
- to evaluate goal maintenance and generalization of skills to different social situations as seen from the teachers' perspective.
- to make and obtain further recommendations for follow-up.
- to determine school peer acceptance over an extended period.

Materials Required

- teachers' goal sheets completed in teacher training sessions
- Teacher Forms REVIEW (Appendix 11)
- Peer Rating Forms (REVIEW) for 7 — 12 year group (Appendix 16)

Procedure

About 1 week prior to review session, group leaders telephone the same teachers as previously to arrange school visits to

1. Obtain feedback from teachers regarding the progress in the school setting of chilren /adolescents who attended the programme.
2. Evaluate goal maintenance in the school setting, and the generalization of skills to different social situations observed by teachers over the three month period since group attendance.
3. Ask teachers to complete Teacher Forms: REVIEW.
4. Make and obtain further recommendations regarding management and goal attainment.
5. Obtain feedback about the utility of the STOP-THINK-DO approach to social problems when applied generally in the classroom and school yard.
7. Peer Rating Forms completed (as discussed in Pre Group Teacher Involvement).

Chapter 7:
Evaluation and Future Directions

The aim in social skills training is to develop empirically based treatment packages which reliably produce significant and maintained improvements in peer relations and social competence of the participants. The social skills training programme outlined in this manual represents an empirically based treatment programme which produces positive, sustained outcomes for children and adolescents, measured at the general impact level, by incorporating in training the major influences in the child's life.

An indication for further programme development concerns the level and methods of assessment/evaluation used. The general impact level utilizing the viewpoints of the child's social contacts is a global method of assessing social skills and change following intervention. It does not specify the exact skills for training. Assessment at the specifying impact level (Kendall et al, 1981) utilizes techniques which enable such precise identification of deficits. This has implications for individual planning of specific remedial strategies to overcome social skills deficits, and would supplement general impact measures.

A useful method of assessment at the specifying level includes observational techniques focussing on discrete behaviours during peer interaction in the natural environment. A formalized example of a descriptive observational method is the Class Play Method of Peer Assessment (Masten et al, 1985). This incorporates observation and measurement of behavioural responses and choices reflecting peer acceptance in specifically devised interpersonal situations.

A further level of assessment requiring consideration is the clinical impact level, which refers to the extent to which the child has been brought within the normal or non-clinical range of functioning as a result of treatment intervention (Kazdin, 1987). By incorporating standardized measures such as the Achenbach Child Behaviour Checklist which discriminates the clinical and non-clinical populations, the efficacy of the treatment programme in relation to its clinical impact may be determined. With the utilization of specifying and clinical impact levels of measurement, the issue regarding the suitability of various clinical populations to the treatment programme could be more formally considered.

Following on this discussion of programme evaluation, consideration should be given to the influence on outcomes of **significant factors in the practical implementation of the programmes**, which are discussed below.

A major factor involves the commitment of group leaders to the empirical basis of the programme, and their ability to transmit and consistently apply information in a supportive, non-judgemental manner within the affective group environment.

Furthermore, the co-operation and involvement of parents and teachers is crucial to provide a broader base for transfer and maintenance of positive outcomes of the intervention programme. The minimum requirement is passive co-operation and the absence of antagonistic environmental influences which will extinguish gains made.

Further practical factors affecting outcome relate to the comprehensiveness of the programme. The critical elements within the programme package are interrelated. Therefore, the efficacy of the programme may be jeopardized if sections or components are omitted. Moreover, since the training programme is a comprehensive and intensive therapeutic intervention, it is offered over a short period of time in the life of a child, adolescent and family. A useful adjunct to the programme may be the provision of subsequent booster sessions for the participants, e.g. 1 session every 6 months to consolidate skill development and acquisition.

In some situations, there are limiting factors on maintenance and transfer of positive outcomes. For example, problems may be encountered with the maintenance of gains in the school situation due to factors such as resistant peer attitudes to the target child, unskilled school peers, or failure by the teacher to adapt the programme effectively in the classroom. Consideration may be given to direct training of school peers by group leaders in the school environment.

Additionally, if children or adolescents show reluctance to practice skills and apply the knowledge gained through the therapeutic experience, they may be encouraged to pursue opportunities for practice in the natural environment. Engaging them in formal direct training of younger children in a school or community setting, along the lines of peer instruction for teaching academic skills may foster transfer and maintenance in the natural environment.

The broad-based, multi-faceted nature of the social skills training package presented in this manual accesses a multitude of resources enabling the provision of ongoing support to children and adolescents in the development of social competence and healthy peer, family, school and community relations.

Appendices
Bibliography

Appendices

Appendix 1

SOCIAL SKILLS TRAINING PROGRAMME
Referral Form

Name: _____ D.O.B.: _____

Address: _____ Telephone: _____

Completed by: _____

Date Completed: _____

1. Reason for referral to a Social Skills Group.

_____

_____

_____

2. Please rate the child on the following scales:-
   Is the child:—
   1) accepted or liked by peers?   **Not at all/Somewhat/Very**
   2) attention seeking/demanding?   **Not at all/Somewhat/Very**
   3) physically aggressive?   **Not at all/Somewhat/Very**
   4) verbally aggressive?   **Not at all/Somewhat/Very**
   5) withdrawn, shy, lacking confidence?   **Not at all/Somewhat/Very**
   6) unable to cope with teasing?   **Not at all/Somewhat/Very**
   7) immature for age?   **Not at all/Somewhat/Very**
   8) having difficulty making or keeping friends?   **Not at all/Somewhat/Very**

3. What goals would you like this child to achieve by attending the group?

_____

_____

_____

Thank you for your referral. We will let you know when the child has been offered a place in the group. At the completion of the group we will forward a summary of the progress made. We anticipate that you will review the child at this stage.

Appendix   2

SOCIAL SKILLS TRAINING PROGRAMME
Waiting List

	NAME	D.O.B.	DATE REFERRED	AGE	REFERRED BY	PREFERRED ATTENDANCE TIME
1						
2						
3						
4						
5						
6						
7						
8						
9						
10						
11						
12						
13						
14						
15						
16						
17						
18						
19						

Appendix   3

SOCIAL SKILLS TRAINING PROGRAMME
Invitation to Attend

Name: Co-ordinator of Social Skills
Programme

Address:

Telephone:

Date:

Parents' name:
Address:

Dear Mr/Ms.

re: Child/Adolescent's name

A group training programme will be provided for children who are having difficulties in social relationships. *(Referring person)* will have mentioned this group to you previously. There will be ten (10) two (2) hour sessions. These sessions will be held on *(day)* from   a.m./p.m. to   a.m./p.m. commencing on *(day, date of first session).*

Parents are required to attend the sessions with their children. At the same time as the children meet in their group, the parents will meet to discuss ways of helping the children to improve their social skills and relationship with others. If parents agree, the teachers of the children will also be involved to help social relationships at school.

As these groups require considerable time and effort committed to them we need to know by *(date)* whether you will be attending the groups. Children and parents who miss any of the sessions will reduce their benefit from the programme. We would like you to commit yourself to attending all sessions.

Please contact us if you have any queries about the group. If you wish, we can send you an information booklet to further explain what the social skills group will be like.

Yours sincerely,

Co-ordinator

Appendix 4

SOCIAL SKILLS TRAINING PROGRAMMME

Information Booklet For Children And Parents

The following is an example of an information booklet explaining the programme to children and parents prior to group attendance. The booklet may be sent to the referring person to pass on to the parent/child, especially if there is some reluctance to attend.

Two texts are presented on each double page, a typed text for parents on the left and, on the right, a text for children in a child's handwriting.

The child's text requires several photos illustrating the various stages in the Social Skills training programme.

Parent Text
(typed)

Page 1

Many children have difficulties in social situations; some are shy, some are aggressive and others are the victims of teasing. When children have difficulties relating to other children, they are often unhappy. Their schoolwork may suffer and their behaviour at home and school may deteriorate.

Child Text
(handwritten)

Page 2

Ben hasn't many friends. He has tried to join in games but is often told to get lost. He sees other children playing together and having fun.

(photo)

Parent Text
(typed)

Page 3

When children are unhappy or in trouble, parents often try to help by offering suggestions to them (e.g. "why don't you play with Lisa instead" or "if you weren't so rough, children would play with you"). However, despite their best intentions, their suggestions are ignored or they are even abused. It is true that children need to learn to think for themselves and solve their own problems. By practicing with a group of children they are more likely to get on with others, and find out for themselves the best way to behave, rather than being told. This is the aim of the Social Skills Group.

Child Text
(handwritten)

Page 4

Ben's mum sees him upset and asks "What's the matter?"
"No-one will play with me." answers Ben. Mum gives Ben ideas on how to make friends. "They don't work!" he says, beginning to get mad. Mum has another idea. She has heard of a group that could help Ben make friends.

(photo)

Parent Text
(typed)

Page 5

The Social Skills Group meets weekly for 2 hours over a 10 week period. Groups are held in a playroom and usually consist of about 6 — 8 children of around the same age, with two

Child Text
(handwritten)

Page 6

It is the day of the group's first meeting. Ben is a bit scared because he doesn't know what will happen. He sees other children waiting with their parents. The children are asked to meet in

group leaders. Parents/caregivers are required to attend a parent group, which is run at the same time. The parents learn ways of helping the children to improve their social skills and relationships with others.

the social skills group room. The parents meet for their group in another room.

(photo)

Parent Text
(typed)
Page 7

Children in the group quickly learn that they are not alone in having difficulty with other children. The groups cater for shy, withdrawn children, noisy, domineering children, rough, aggressive children, and immature children. The group leaders are well trained in the management of such children

Each session is divided into two sections. In the first the focus is on directly teaching social skills, and in the second, the children practice these through play.

Child Text
(handwritten)
Page 8

Ben meets the other children in the group. He is surprised to learn that they have trouble making friends too, but for different reasons.

Jason tries to act tough. He pushes other kids around.

Michael tells tales. The other children call him "Dobber".

Alison also tells tales and often acts silly.

David is so shy, he sits in the corner and doesn't speak.

Jane is also shy and can't stand up for herself.

John can't stop talking. He interrupts all the time and yells at people.

(photo)

Parent Text
(typed)
Page 9

In the groups, social skills are taught in practical ways, using methods that will interest and motivate children, for example by using videos, games, group activities and plays. They are given opportunities to apply what they have learned in the group and also encouraged to practice their new skills at home and school.

Child Text
(handwritten)
Page 10

During the next few weeks, Ben had lots of fun. He played games, watched cartoons and talked to the other children. He also made up plays and acted in them.

(photo)

Parent Text
(typed)
Page 11

The motto of the group is "STOP, THINK, DO". Children who have trouble relating to others do not usually think about why they have the problem or how they should handle it. They just act on impulse or habit, often with unpleasant consequences. The major focus of the Social Skills programme is to teach children to:

Child Text
(handwritten)
Page 12

Ben learned many things. He could tell how others were feeling, and explain his own feelings. He learnt how to be a better friend. He could solve problems for himself by thinking. To remind him of this, he made a traffic light badge that showed STOP, THINK, DO. Each week, Ben did homework to practice what he had learnt in the group. He won a prize for this.

STOP - when they have a problem with other people.

THINK -about alternative ways of solving those problems, and choose the best solution.

DO - it.

As a part of the problem solving process, they learn to recognize and express the different feelings of others and think about the possible consequences of their actions.

In their weekly homework exercises, children are encouraged to practice their group skills at school and home.

(photo)

Parent Text
(typed)

Page 13

Other essential components of the programme include fostering co-operation, sharing, communication and decision making between the children, not as individuals but group members. The final farewell party, planned and directed by the children as a group, emphasizes these aspects of the Social Skills programme.

Child Text
(handwritten)

Page 14

The children learned to share and co-operate with each other. Ben had fun doing this. In the last week, the children co-operated in planning their farewell party. Ben was a little sad to say good-bye to his new friends in the group.

(photo)

Parent Text
(typed)

Page 15

The group leaders maintain contact with parents and teachers assisting them to apply the problem solving principles.

Child Text
(handwritten)

Page 16

Now when Ben has a problem with his friends he remembers the motto "STOP, THINK, DO". By practicing this motto he can solve his own problems. At school, Ben has made more friends and feels happier.

(photo)

Page 17

The Social Skills Groups are held during school terms, with groups meeting once a week for 10 weeks. Each session lasts 2 hours. Children are grouped together according to their age.

Referrals can be made by contacting the Co-ordinator, Social Skills Training Programme, Address......... Telephone..........

A parent/caregiver is required to attend a parent training group which is run at the same time. If the parent agrees, the child's teacher is also involved in the programme to help improve social relationships at school.

Appendix 5

SOCIAL SKILLS TRAINING PROGRAMME
Parent Form: PRE GROUP

Child's Name: _____ Date: _____

Address: _____ Telephone: _____

Age: _____ Date of Birth: _____

Name of Parent(s) Attending: _____

School: _____ Year: _____

Teacher's Name: _____

Permission to Contact Teacher: Yes/No

Permission to video the children's group for use in teaching professional staff and students, not for public viewing. The children will not be identified in any way by name or address:

Yes/No   Signature: _____

Please tick the appropriate box:

IS YOUR CHILD:—

1. **ACCEPTED OR LIKED BY PEERS?**

   [   ]   [   ]   [   ]   [   ]   [   ]
   Not at all   Slightly   Somewhat   Moderately   Very

2. **ATTENTION-SEEKING/DEMANDING?**

   [   ]   [   ]   [   ]   [   ]   [   ]
   Not at all   Slightly   Somewhat   Moderately   Very

3. **PHYSICALLY AGGRESSIVE?**

   [   ]   [   ]   [   ]   [   ]   [   ]
   Not at all   Slightly   Somewhat   Moderately   Very

4. **VERBALLY AGGRESSIVE?**

   [   ]   [   ]   [   ]   [   ]   [   ]
   Not at all   Slightly   Somewhat   Moderately   Very

5. **WITHDRAWN, SHY, LACKING CONFIDENCE?**

[ ]	[ ]	[ ]	[ ]	[ ]
Not at all	Slightly	Somewhat	Moderately	Very

6. **UNABLE TO COPE WITH TEASING?**

[ ]	[ ]	[ ]	[ ]	[ ]
Not at all	Slightly	Somewhat	Moderately	Very

7. **IMMATURE FOR AGE?**

[ ]	[ ]	[ ]	[ ]	[ ]
Not at all	Slightly	Somewhat	Moderately	Very

8. **HAVING DIFFICULTY MAKING FRIENDS?**

[ ]	[ ]	[ ]	[ ]	[ ]
Not at all	Slightly	Somewhat	Moderately	Very

9. **HAVING DIFFICULTY KEEPING FRIENDS?**

[ ]	[ ]	[ ]	[ ]	[ ]
Not at all	Slightly	Somewhat	Moderately	Very

10. **HAVING LEARNING PROBLEMS?**

[ ]	[ ]	[ ]	[ ]	[ ]
Not at all	Slight	Somewhat	Moderate	Extreme

11. **WHAT GOALS WOULD YOU LIKE YOUR CHILD TO ACHIEVE BY ATTENDING THE GROUP?**

_____

_____

12. **WHAT GOALS WOULD YOU LIKE TO ACHIEVE YOURSELF BY ATTENDING THE GROUP?**

_____

13. **WHAT ARE SOME POSITIVE AND PROMISING ASPECTS OF YOUR CHILD?**

_____

_____

Appendix   6

SOCIAL SKILLS TRAINING PROGRAMME
Parent Form: POST GROUP

Child's Name: _____ Date: _____

Name of Parent(s) Attending: _____

Please tick the appropriate box:

IS YOUR CHILD:—

1. **ACCEPTED OR LIKED BY PEERS?**

    [   ]   [   ]   [   ]   [   ]   [   ]
    Not at all   Slightly   Somewhat   Moderately   Very

2. **ATTENTION-SEEKING/DEMANDING?**

    [   ]   [   ]   [   ]   [   ]   [   ]
    Not at all   Slightly   Somewhat   Moderately   Very

3. **PHYSICALLY AGGRESSIVE?**

    [   ]   [   ]   [   ]   [   ]   [   ]
    Not at all   Slightly   Somewhat   Moderately   Very

4. **VERBALLY AGGRESSIVE?**

    [   ]   [   ]   [   ]   [   ]   [   ]
    Not at all   Slightly   Somewhat   Moderately   Very

5. **WITHDRAWN, SHY, LACKING CONFIDENCE?**

    [   ]   [   ]   [   ]   [   ]   [   ]
    Not at all   Slightly   Somewhat   Moderately   Very

6. **UNABLE TO COPE WITH TEASING?**

    [   ]   [   ]   [   ]   [   ]   [   ]
    Not at all   Slightly   Somewhat   Moderately   Very

7. IMMATURE FOR AGE?

[   ]   [   ]   [   ]   [   ]   [   ]
Not at all   Slightly   Somewhat   Moderately   Very

8. HAVING DIFFICULTY MAKING FRIENDS?

[   ]   [   ]   [   ]   [   ]   [   ]
Not at all   Slightly   Somewhat   Moderately   Very

9. HAVING DIFFICULTY KEEPING FRIENDS?

[   ]   [   ]   [   ]   [   ]   [   ]
Not at all   Slightly   Somewhat   Moderately   Very

10. HAVING LEARNING PROBLEMS?

[   ]   [   ]   [   ]   [   ]   [   ]
Not at all   Slight   Somewhat   Moderate   Extreme

11. WHAT GOALS HAS YOUR CHILD ACHIEVED BY ATTENDING THE GROUP?

_____

_____

_____

12. WHAT GOALS HAVE YOU ACHIEVED YOURSELF BY ATTENDING THE GROUP?

_____

_____

_____

_____

_____

_____

_____

_____

Appendix 7

SOCIAL SKILLS TRAINING PROGRAMME
Parent Form: REVIEW

Child's Name: _____ Date: _____

Name of Parent(s) Attending: _____

Please tick the appropriate box:

IS YOUR CHILD:—

1. ACCEPTED OR LIKED BY PEERS?

[   ]   [   ]   [   ]   [   ]   [   ]
Not at all   Slightly   Somewhat   Moderately   Very

2. ATTENTION-SEEKING/DEMANDING?

[   ]   [   ]   [   ]   [   ]   [   ]
Not at all   Slightly   Somewhat   Moderately   Very

3. PHYSICALLY AGGRESSIVE?

[   ]   [   ]   [   ]   [   ]   [   ]
Not at all   Slightly   Somewhat   Moderately   Very

4. VERBALLY AGGRESSIVE?

[   ]   [   ]   [   ]   [   ]   [   ]
Not at all   Slightly   Somewhat   Moderately   Very

5. WITHDRAWN, SHY, LACKING CONFIDENCE?

[   ]   [   ]   [   ]   [   ]   [   ]
Not at all   Slightly   Somewhat   Moderately   Very

6. UNABLE TO COPE WITH TEASING?

[   ]   [   ]   [   ]   [   ]   [   ]
Not at all   Slightly   Somewhat   Moderately   Very

7. **IMMATURE FOR AGE?**

[　]   [　]   [　]   [　]   [　]
Not at all   Slightly   Somewhat   Moderately   Very

8. **HAVING DIFFICULTY MAKING FRIENDS?**

[　]   [　]   [　]   [　]   [　]
Not at all   Slightly   Somewhat   Moderately   Very

9. **HAVING DIFFICULTY KEEPING FRIENDS?**

[　]   [　]   [　]   [　]   [　]
Not at all   Slightly   Somewhat   Moderately   Very

10. **HAVING LEARNING PROBLEMS?**

[　]   [　]   [　]   [　]   [　]
Not at all   Slight   Somewhat   Moderate   Extreme

11. **WHICH GOALS YOUR CHILD ACHIEVED IN THE GROUP HAVE BEEN MAINTAINED?**

_____

_____

_____

12. **WHICH GOALS YOU YOURSELF ACHIEVED IN THE GROUP HAVE BEEN MAINTAINED?**

_____

_____

_____

13. **WHAT OTHER GOALS WOULD YOU LIKE YOUR CHILD TO ACHIEVE?**

_____

_____

_____

_____

Appendix 8
SOCIAL SKILLS TRAINING PROGRAMME
General Information Leaflet

REFERRALS

Children are referred to the Social Skills Training Programme because of difficulties with interpersonal relationships. They range from socially withdrawn or shy children to verbally and physically aggressive children. Frequently the children are unable to cope with teasing or alternatively initiate teasing of others. Some children behave immaturely while others are attention-seeking and demanding. Generally, they have difficulty making and maintaining friendships with peers. The groups do not cater for children with more severe behaviour problems. Children are referred to the programme co-ordinator by people involved with the child or adolescent, in liaison with parents.

CHILD/ADOLESCENT GROUPS

Generally, one social skills group is run each school term. The groups, each consisting of 6 — 8 children are formed roughly on an age basis 7 — 9 year olds, 10 — 12 year olds and 13 — 15 year olds. The group for each term runs for a 10 week period, and is held once a week for 2 hours.

PARENT INVOLVEMENT

It is required that parents attend a concurrent parent group each week. They receive continual feedback about the children's progress within the child/adolescent group and offer feedback about home progress. The parents are also instructed in the STOP-THINK-DO approach to social problem solving, and are encouraged to use and assist their child to practice newly learned social skills in the home environment.

TEACHER INVOLVEMENT

Teachers are contacted by telephone to arrange visits to the school early in the group, and at its conclusion. During the term, they are also invited to attend Teacher Training Sessions where they are instructed in the STOP-THINK-DO method. They are encouraged to reinforce the children's newly learned social skills in the school environment.

AIMS

Specifically, the aims of the Social Skills Training Programme are to teach children and adolescents:—

- to meet and get to know people
- to recognize feelings in themselves and others
- to express and communicate feelings appropriately
- to think before acting
- to solve social problems using a step by step cognitive "thinking" approach
- to evaluate behaviour in terms of consequences
- to practice new skills in a safe, supportive environment
- to foster self-confidence
- to motivate the child to achieve personal and socially acceptable goals in social interactions
- to participate and co-operate in a group situation
- to encourage the extension of these skills into the home and school through the direct involvement of parents and teachers in the training programme

FORMAT

Generally, each social skills session has 2 major components — a structured component involving videos, discussion, roleplays, problem-solving exercises and direct teaching of principles; and an informal component where children are involved in free play to practice and apply these principles under the guidance of the group leaders. The groups for adolescents are flexible and usually involve more informal discussion and practice in real-life situations. Children complete homework exercises each week to aid in learning and application of social skills acquired in the group.

The format of the parent and teacher training groups is also flexible with each session involving instruction and practice in social problem-solving principles, communication skills and ways of helping the children improve their social relationships.

STOP-THINK-DO

One of the main components of the programme is the teaching of the STOP-THINK-DO approach to social problem solving to the children, parents and teachers alike. The approach is introduced using a traffic light motto i.e.:—

STOP	Reminds the children to stop before they rush into anything, consider the problem and how they and others are feeling, and what they want to happen in the situation.
THINK	Reminds the children to think about and generate many possible alternative solutions to the problem.

Solutions may involve

- fighting/forcing
- telling an adult
- demanding
- asking nicely
- bargaining
- sharing/compromising
- walking away

Then, think of the consequences of each solution and how the people involved may feel about the consequences.

DO	Reminds the children to finally choose the best solution (i.e. the one with the most acceptable consequences) and put it into action to solve their own social problem. If this solution does not work, go back to STOP and work through as above.

Children are encouraged to apply this principle to all social problems e.g. being the victim of teasing, having no-one to play with, not being allowed to do what they want by parents or teachers, responding to peer pressure.

REVIEW

A three month follow-up meeting is arranged to review the children's progress. Further recommendations are made as required.

Appendix 9

SOCIAL SKILLS TRAINING PROGRAMME
Teacher Form: PRE GROUP

Child's Name: _____

Age: _____ Date: _____

School: _____ Grade: _____ Phone: _____

School Address: _____

Teacher's Name: _____

Please tick the appropriate box:

IS THE CHILD:—

1. **ACCEPTED OR LIKED BY PEERS?**

   [   ]   [   ]   [   ]   [   ]   [   ]
   Not at all   Slightly   Somewhat   Moderately   Very

2. **ATTENTION-SEEKING/DEMANDING?**

   [   ]   [   ]   [   ]   [   ]   [   ]
   Not at all   Slightly   Somewhat   Moderately   Very

3. **PHYSICALLY AGGRESSIVE?**

   [   ]   [   ]   [   ]   [   ]   [   ]
   Not at all   Slightly   Somewhat   Moderately   Very

4. **VERBALLY AGGRESSIVE?**

   [   ]   [   ]   [   ]   [   ]   [   ]
   Not at all   Slightly   Somewhat   Moderately   Very

5. **WITHDRAWN, SHY, LACKING CONFIDENCE?**

   [   ]   [   ]   [   ]   [   ]   [   ]
   Not at all   Slightly   Somewhat   Moderately   Very

6. UNABLE TO COPE WITH TEASING?

[   ]   [   ]   [   ]   [   ]   [   ]
Not at all   Slightly   Somewhat   Moderately   Very

7. IMMATURE FOR AGE?

[   ]   [   ]   [   ]   [   ]   [   ]
Not at all   Slightly   Somewhat   Moderately   Very

8. HAVING DIFFICULTY MAKING FRIENDS?

[   ]   [   ]   [   ]   [   ]   [   ]
Not at all   Slightly   Somewhat   Moderately   Very

9. HAVING DIFFICULTY KEEPING FRIENDS?

[   ]   [   ]   [   ]   [   ]   [   ]
Not at all   Slightly   Somewhat   Moderately   Very

10. HAVING LEARNING PROBLEMS?

[   ]   [   ]   [   ]   [   ]   [   ]
Not at all   Slight   Somewhat   Moderate   Extreme

11. WHAT GOALS WOULD YOU LIKE THIS CHILD TO ACHIEVE BY ATTENDING THE GROUP?

_____

_____

_____

12. WHAT ARE SOME POSITIVE AND PROMISING ASPECTS OF THIS CHILD?

_____

_____

_____

_____

Appendix 10

SOCIAL SKILLS TRAINING PROGRAMME
Teacher Form: POST GROUP

Child's Name: _____ Date: _____

Age: _____

Teacher's Name: _____

Please tick the appropriate box:

IS THE CHILD:—

1. **ACCEPTED OR LIKED BY PEERS?**

   [   ]   [   ]   [   ]   [   ]   [   ]
   Not at all   Slightly   Somewhat   Moderately   Very

2. **ATTENTION-SEEKING/DEMANDING?**

   [   ]   [   ]   [   ]   [   ]   [   ]
   Not at all   Slightly   Somewhat   Moderately   Very

3. **PHYSICALLY AGGRESSIVE?**

   [   ]   [   ]   [   ]   [   ]   [   ]
   Not at all   Slightly   Somewhat   Moderately   Very

4. **VERBALLY AGGRESSIVE?**

   [   ]   [   ]   [   ]   [   ]   [   ]
   Not at all   Slightly   Somewhat   Moderately   Very

5. **WITHDRAWN, SHY, LACKING CONFIDENCE?**

   [   ]   [   ]   [   ]   [   ]   [   ]
   Not at all   Slightly   Somewhat   Moderately   Very

6. UNABLE TO COPE WITH TEASING?

[   ]   [   ]   [   ]   [   ]   [   ]
Not at all   Slightly   Somewhat   Moderately   Very

7. IMMATURE FOR AGE?

[   ]   [   ]   [   ]   [   ]   [   ]
Not at all   Slightly   Somewhat   Moderately   Very

8. HAVING DIFFICULTY MAKING FRIENDS?

[   ]   [   ]   [   ]   [   ]   [   ]
Not at all   Slightly   Somewhat   Moderately   Very

9. HAVING DIFFICULTY KEEPING FRIENDS?

[   ]   [   ]   [   ]   [   ]   [   ]
Not at all   Slightly   Somewhat   Moderately   Very

10. HAVING LEARNING PROBLEMS?

[   ]   [   ]   [   ]   [   ]   [   ]
Not at all   Slight   Somewhat   Moderate   Extreme

11. WHAT GOALS HAS THE CHILD ACHIEVED BY ATTENDING THE GROUP?

_____

_____

_____

Appendix   11

SOCIAL SKILLS TRAINING PROGRAMME
Teacher Form: REVIEW

Child's Name: _____ Date: _____

Age: _____

Teacher's Name: _____

Please tick the appropriate box:

IS THE CHILD:—

1.   ACCEPTED OR LIKED BY PEERS?

[   ]   [   ]   [   ]   [   ]   [   ]
Not at all   Slightly   Somewhat   Moderately   Very

2.   ATTENTION-SEEKING/DEMANDING?

[   ]   [   ]   [   ]   [   ]   [   ]
Not at all   Slightly   Somewhat   Moderately   Very

3.   PHYSICALLY AGGRESSIVE?

[   ]   [   ]   [   ]   [   ]   [   ]
Not at all   Slightly   Somewhat   Moderately   Very

4.   VERBALLY AGGRESSIVE?

[   ]   [   ]   [   ]   [   ]   [   ]
Not at all   Slightly   Somewhat   Moderately   Very

5.   WITHDRAWN, SHY, LACKING CONFIDENCE?

[   ]   [   ]   [   ]   [   ]   [   ]
Not at all   Slightly   Somewhat   Moderately   Very

6.   UNABLE TO COPE WITH TEASING?

[   ]   [   ]   [   ]   [   ]   [   ]
Not at all   Slightly   Somewhat   Moderately   Very

7. IMMATURE FOR AGE?

[   ]   [   ]   [   ]   [   ]   [   ]
Not at all   Slightly   Somewhat   Moderately   Very

8. HAVING DIFFICULTY MAKING FRIENDS?

[   ]   [   ]   [   ]   [   ]   [   ]
Not at all   Slightly   Somewhat   Moderately   Very

9. HAVING DIFFICULTY KEEPING FRIENDS?

[   ]   [   ]   [   ]   [   ]   [   ]
Not at all   Slightly   Somewhat   Moderately   Very

10. HAVING LEARNING PROBLEMS?

[   ]   [   ]   [   ]   [   ]   [   ]
Not at all   Slight   Somewhat   Moderate   Extreme

11. WHICH GOALS THE CHILD ACHIEVED IN THE GROUP HAVE BEEN MAINTAINED?

_____

_____

_____

12. WHAT OTHER GOALS WOULD YOU LIKE THE CHILD TO ACHIEVE?

_____

_____

_____

Appendix 12

SOCIAL SKILLS GROUP TRAINING PROGRAMME
Self Report Form: PRE GROUP

Child's Name: _____

Age: _____

Date: _____

Please tick the box that is true for you:

1. **HOW MUCH ARE YOU LIKED BY OTHER KIDS?**

   [   ]   [   ]   [   ]   [   ]
   Not at all   A little bit   Quite a lot   Heaps

2. **DO YOU FIGHT WITH OTHER KIDS?**

   [   ]   [   ]   [   ]   [   ]
   Not at all   A little bit   Quite a lot   Heaps

3. **ARE YOU SHY WITH OTHER KIDS?**

   [   ]   [   ]   [   ]   [   ]
   Not at all   A little bit   Quite a lot   Heaps

4. **DOES TEASING UPSET YOU?**

   [   ]   [   ]   [   ]   [   ]
   Not at all   A little bit   Quite a lot   Heaps

5. **IS IT HARD FOR YOU TO MAKE FRIENDS?**

   [   ]   [   ]   [   ]   [   ]
   Not at all   A little bit   Quite a lot   Heaps

6. **IS IT HARD FOR YOU TO KEEP YOUR FRIENDS?**

   [   ]   [   ]   [   ]   [   ]
   Not at all   A little bit   Quite a lot   Heaps

7. **DO YOU HAVE PROBLEMS WITH LEARNING AT SCHOOL?**

    [ ]   [ ]   [ ]   [ ]
  Not at all   A little bit   Quite a lot   Heaps

8. **WHAT GOALS WOULD YOU LIKE TO ACHIEVE BY COMING TO THE GROUP?**

_____

_____

_____

9. **WHAT THINGS DO YOU LIKE DOING BEST?**

_____

_____

_____

SOCIAL SKILLS GROUP TRAINING PROGRAMME
Self Report Form: POST GROUP

Child's Name: _____ Date: _____

Please tick the box that is true for you:

1. HOW MUCH ARE YOU LIKED BY OTHER KIDS?

[   ]   [   ]   [   ]   [   ]
Not at all   A little bit   Quite a lot   Heaps

2. DO YOU FIGHT WITH OTHER KIDS?

[   ]   [   ]   [   ]   [   ]
Not at all   A little bit   Quite a lot   Heaps

3. ARE YOU SHY WITH OTHER KIDS?

[   ]   [   ]   [   ]   [   ]
Not at all   A little bit   Quite a lot   Heaps

4. DOES TEASING UPSET YOU?

[   ]   [   ]   [   ]   [   ]
Not at all   A little bit   Quite a lot   Heaps

5. IS IT HARD FOR YOU TO MAKE FRIENDS?

[   ]   [   ]   [   ]   [   ]
Not at all   A little bit   Quite a lot   Heaps

6. IS IT HARD FOR YOU TO KEEP YOUR FRIENDS?

[   ]   [   ]   [   ]   [   ]
Not at all   A little bit   Quite a lot   Heaps

7. DO YOU HAVE PROBLEMS WITH LEARNING AT SCHOOL?

[   ]   [   ]   [   ]   [   ]
Not at all   A little bit   Quite a lot   Heaps

8.   WHAT GOALS HAVE YOU ACHIEVED BY COMING TO THE GROUP?

_____

_____

_____

Appendix 14

SOCIAL SKILLS TRAINING PROGRAMME
Self Report Form: REVIEW

Child's Name: _____ Date: _____

Please tick the box that is true for you:

1. **HOW MUCH ARE YOU LIKED BY OTHER KIDS?**

   [   ]   [   ]   [   ]   [   ]
   Not at all   A little bit   Quite a lot   Heaps

2. **DO YOU FIGHT WITH OTHER KIDS?**

   [   ]   [   ]   [   ]   [   ]
   Not at all   A little bit   Quite a lot   Heaps

3. **ARE YOU SHY WITH OTHER KIDS?**

   [   ]   [   ]   [   ]   [   ]
   Not at all   A little bit   Quite a lot   Heaps

4. **DOES TEASING UPSET YOU?**

   [   ]   [   ]   [   ]   [   ]
   Not at all   A little bit   Quite a lot   Heaps

5. **IS IT HARD FOR YOU TO MAKE FRIENDS?**

   [   ]   [   ]   [   ]   [   ]
   Not at all   A little bit   Quite a lot   Heaps

6. **IS IT HARD FOR YOU TO KEEP YOUR FRIENDS?**

   [   ]   [   ]   [   ]   [   ]
   Not at all   A little bit   Quite a lot   Heaps

7. **DO YOU HAVE PROBLEMS WITH LEARNING AT SCHOOL?**

   [   ]   [   ]   [   ]   [   ]
   Not at all   A little bit   Quite a lot   Heaps

8. WHICH GOALS YOU ACHIEVED IN THE GROUP ARE STILL GOING OK?

_____
_____
_____
_____
_____
_____
_____
_____
_____
_____

9. WHAT OTHER GOALS WOULD YOU LIKE TO ACHIEVE?

_____
_____
_____
_____
_____
_____
_____
_____
_____
_____
_____
_____
_____

Appendix   15
SOCIAL SKILLS PROGRAMME EVALUATION REPORT

Name: _____ Date: _____

1. **GROUP LEADER'S REPORT**

   Goals Set __ _____

   _____

   _____

   Goals Achieved _____

   _____

   _____

2. **PARENT'S REPORT**

   Goals Set _____

   _____

   _____

   Goals Achieved _____

   _____

   _____

3. **TEACHER'S REPORT**

   Goals Set _____

   _____

   _____

   Goals Achieved _____

   _____

   _____

4. **PEER RATINGS** *(IF APPLICABLE)* _____

   _____

   _____

5. **RECOMMENDATIONS** _____

   _____

   _____

SOCIAL SKILLS TRAINING PROGRAMME
Peer Rating Form: PRE/POST/REVIEW

Please tick one of the following that is true for you:

1.   How much do you play with

_____	[ ] Not at all	[ ] A little bit	[ ] Quite a lot	[ ] Heaps
_____	[ ] Not at all	[ ] A little bit	[ ] Quite a lot	[ ] Heaps
_____	[ ] Not at all	[ ] A little bit	[ ] Quite a lot	[ ] Heaps
_____	[ ] Not at all	[ ] A little bit	[ ] Quite a lot	[ ] Heaps
_____	[ ] Not at all	[ ] A little bit	[ ] Quite a lot	[ ] Heaps

2.   How much do you like

_____	[ ] Not at all	[ ] A little bit	[ ] Quite a lot	[ ] Heaps
_____	[ ] Not at all	[ ] A little bit	[ ] Quite a lot	[ ] Heaps
_____	[ ] Not at all	[ ] A little bit	[ ] Quite a lot	[ ] Heaps
_____	[ ] Not at all	[ ] A little bit	[ ] Quite a lot	[ ] Heaps
_____	[ ] Not at all	[ ] A little bit	[ ] Quite a lot	[ ] Heaps

3. Is .... your friend?

——————————   [   ]   [   ]   [   ]   [   ]
              Not at all   A bit of a friend   A good friend   A best friend

——————————   [   ]   [   ]   [   ]   [   ]
              Not at all   A bit of a friend   A good friend   A best friend

——————————   [   ]   [   ]   [   ]   [   ]
              Not at all   A bit of a friend   A good friend   A best friend

——————————   [   ]   [   ]   [   ]   [   ]
              Not at all   A bit of a friend   A good friend   A best friend

——————————   [   ]   [   ]   [   ]   [   ]
              Not at all   A bit of a friend   A good friend   A best friend

Appendix   17

SOCIAL SKILLS TRAINING PROGRAMME
Review Letter

Name: Co-ordinator of Social Skills
Programme

Address:

Telephone:

Date:

Parents' name:
Address:

Dear Mr/ Ms. *(Parent)* and *(Child/ Adolescent)*

You are reminded of the Review Meeting for the Social Skills Training group which you attended three months ago.

This meeting will be held on *(day), (date)* from   a.m./ p.m. to   a.m./ p.m..

Children and parents are asked to attend. The teachers who were involved in the training programme will be contacted prior to the review meeting to discuss progress at school.

Please let us know by *(date)* whether you will be attending the review meeting.

Yours sincerely,

Co-ordinator

Appendix 18

SOCIAL SKILLS TRAINING PROGRAMME
STOP-THINK-DO Posters

Poster Tracing the STOP-THINK-DO problem solving sequence using a traffic light motto.

Appendix 19, 20

SOCIAL SKILLS TRAINING PROGRAMME
COOL/WEAK/AGGRO; Purposes of Misbehaviour Posters

cool, weak OR *aggro* **WAYS TO BEHAVE**

	4 PURPOSES OF MISBEHAVIOUR *	
CHILD'S PURPOSE	CHILD'S BEHAVIOUR	PARENT'S FEELING AND REACTION

THE **weak** WAY IS TO:
— talk softly, mumble
— cry or sulk when faced with a problem
— look down at the floor
— stand far away, hunched over
— give in to others
— feel shy, embarrassed, nervous, useless, unhappy

CHILD'S PURPOSE	CHILD'S BEHAVIOUR	PARENT'S FEELING AND REACTION
1. ATTENTION	Shows off, Whines, Dawdles	Angry Gives in to child
2. POWER	Argumentative, Uncooperative	Angry Bosses child or gives in to child
3. RETALIATION OR REVENGE	Gets even, or retaliates; Refuses to cooperate.	Hurt, Angry, Retaliates.
4. INADEQUACY	Unable to cope.	Anxious, Worried. Tries to assist child overcome difficulty.

THE **aggro** WAY IS TO:
— shout, yell
— speak rudely, abuse, tease
— blame others
— look mad
— stand close and threaten
— push, hit kick
— feel angry, annoyed, out of control, put down

THE *cool* WAY IS TO:
— speak firmly but friendly
— stand up for yourself politely
— smile or look calm
— stand tall
— look other person in the eyes
— feel happy, confident, in control, and OK about yourself

*The 4 purposes of misbehaviour were derived by Dreikurs R & Soltz V. HAPPY CHILDREN, A CHALLENGE TO PARENTS, Fontana, Glasgow, 1972.

19. COOL/WEAK/AGGRO *for evaluation of strategies in social problem situations.*

20. Purposes of Misbehaviour *poster used in the parent training programme.*

Appendix 21

SOCIAL SKILLS TRAINING PROGRAMME
Clancy the Clown

Puppet figure with removable faces for demonstrating feeling recognition for younger children.

Appendix 22

PARENT TRAINING PROGRAMME

Overview of Communication and Problem-Solving Strategies

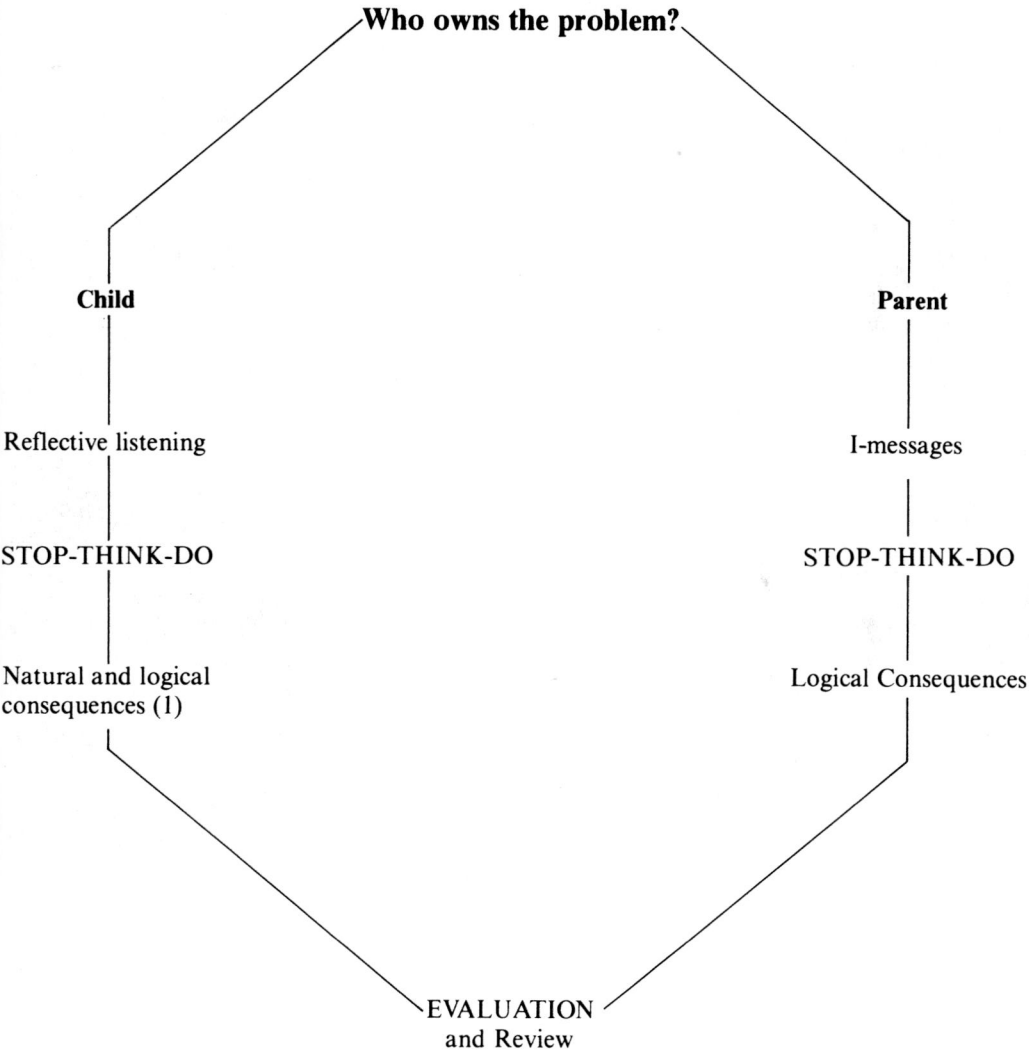

Who owns the problem?

Child

Reflective listening

STOP-THINK-DO

Natural and logical consequences (1)

Parent

I-messages

STOP-THINK-DO

Logical Consequences

EVALUATION
and Review

(1) The term "Natural and Logical Consequences" was derived by Dreikurs R and Soltz V.
(1972) Happy Children. A Challenge to Parents. Glasgow. Fontana.

Appendix 23

PARENT TRAINING PROGRAMME
Observation of Behaviour Exercise

In order to understand and alter if necessary behaviour of those involved in problem situations, it is necessary to observe closely what actually occurs, and consider the need or purpose the behaviour serves.

To practice observation of behaviour, we suggest you use the following headings:

1. What the child/adolescent did.
2. Your feelings.
3. Your reaction.
4. The child/adolescent's response.

Exercise:

Read the following parent-child problem situation.

Parent. *(friendly tone)*:	"Hi, how was school today?"
Child. *(sounding dejected)*:	"Oh, alright I suppose".
Parent:	"What happened?"
Child:	"The teacher's given us heaps of homework, and I can't do it all. It's not fair. I'm not going to do it all. There's too much."
Parent *(in angry tone)*:	"Your grades aren't that good. You'd better get into your room right now and get started on it or you'll be up all night doing it."
Child:	"Ah it's not fair. I don't want to do it."
Parent:	"You get in there now, off you go."
Child:	Reluctantly goes to room.

Now analyse the behaviour of those involved, and record your answers. Check your answer below.

1. What the child did. _____
2. Parent's feelings. _____
3. Parent's reaction. _____
4. Child's response. _____

Appropriate Responses

1. What the child did. **Refused to do homework.**
2. Parent's feelings. **Angry, Worried.**
3. Parent's reaction. **Bossed the Child.**
4. Child's response. **Submitted reluctantly. Dawdled to room.**

220

Appendix 24

PARENT/TEACHER TRAINING PROGRAMME
COOL/WEAK/AGGRO Handout for Parents/Teachers

When encouraging children to THINK about solutions to their social problems, it is useful to categorize the different ways of behaving as follows .....

The COOL way is to :
— speak firmly but friendly
— stand up for yourself politely
— smile or look calm
— stand tall
— look other person in the eyes
— feel happy, confident, in control, okay about yourself.

The WEAK way is to:
— talk softly, mumble
— cry or sulk when faced with a problem
— look down at the floor
— stand far away, hunched over
— give in to others
— feel shy, embarrassed, nervous, useless, unhappy.

The AGGRO way is to:
— shout, yell
— speak rudely, abuse, tease, put down
— blame others
— look mad
— stand close and threaten
— push, hit, kick
— feel angry, annoyed, out of control.

Appendix 25
PARENT/TEACHER TRAINING PROGRAMME
STOP-THINK-DO Handout For Parents/Teachers
(7 — 12 Year Groups)

Plan of action for parents/teachers to mediate in social problem solving with children. The method may be short cut with practice.

STOP _____ **Define Problem**
    Parent/Teacher: — Approaches child(ren)
    — "What is the problem here?"
    Child: — Explains problem.

_____ **Recognize Feelings**
    Parent/Teacher: — "How do you feel about what happened?" or, "I can see you're upset, angry etc."
    Child: — Expresses feelings about problem.

_____ **Identify Goals**
    Parent/Teacher: — "What do you want to happen?"
    Child: — States goals.

THINK _____ **Generate Solutions**
    Parent/Teacher: — "What can you do about it?"
    Offers suggestions in initial stages.
    Child: — Gives alternative solutions.
    Listens to suggestions of others.

_____ **Evaluate Consequences**
    Parent/Teacher: — "What could happen if you did that?"
    Offers suggestions in initial stages.
    "How would you feel about that?"
    Child: — Gives possible consequences.
    Listens to suggestions of others.
    Expresses feelings about consequences.

DO _____ **Choose Solution**
    Parent/Teacher: — "Which way is the best way?"
    Child: — Chooses best solution for all concerned.

_____ **Initiate action**
    Parent/Teacher: — "Go ahead and try it!"
    — "If it doesn't work, think again".
    — Assists child to initiate action if needed.
    — Reinforces child for efforts.
    Child: — Acts to solve the social problem.

Appendix 26
PARENT/TEACHER TRAINING PROGRAMME
STOP-THINK-DO Handout For Parents/Teachers
(Adolescent Groups)

Plan of action for parents/teachers to facilitate social problem solving with adolescents. The method may be short cut with practice.

STOP _____ **Define Problem**
Parent/Teacher: — Approaches adolescent(s) during or after the problem situation
— "You seem to have a problem with ----".
Adolescent: — Confirms, clarifies, rejects this observation.

_____ **Recognize Feelings**
Parent/Teacher: — "I can see you feel angry, upset, frustrated" or, "How do you feel about it?"
Adolescent: — Confirms, clarifies, rejects feeling reflection.

_____ **Identify Goals**
Parent/Teacher: — "What do you want to happen?"
Adolescent: — Clarifies goals.

THINK _____ **Generate Solutions**
Parent/Teacher: — "What can you do about it?"
Offers suggestions in initial stages.
Adolescent: — Gives alternative solutions.
Listens to suggestions of others.

_____ **Evaluate Consequences**
Parent/Teacher: — "What could happen if you did that?"
Offers suggestions in initial stages.
— "How do you feel about that?" or, "Do you want that?"
Adolescent: — Gives possible consequences
Listens to suggestions.
Expresses feelings about consequences.

DO _____ **Choose Solution**
Parent/Teacher: — "Which way will work best?
Adolescent: — Chooses solution with most acceptable consequences.

_____ **Initiate action**
Parent/Teacher: — "Why don't you try it!"
— "I'd like to know how it works out".
— Assists adolescent to initiate action if needed.
— Reinforces adolescent for efforts.
Adolescent: — Acts to solve the social problem.

223

Appendix 27

TEACHER TRAINING PROGRAMME
Evaluation Of STOP-THINK-DO Approach In The School Setting

Teacher's Name: ———————————————————————— Date: ————————————

Child's Name: ——

1. Have you found the STOP-THINK-DO approach useful for you to assist the child in solving social problems more effectively?

    ——

2. Give an example of a situation where you used this method with the child.
    What was the problem? ————————————————————————————————

    ——

    What did you do/say? ——————————————————————————————

    ——

    How did the child respond? ————————————————————————————

    ——

3. What difficulties have you encountered using this method?

    ——

    ——

4. Do you think that the child is learning to use the STOP-THINK-DO method him/her self? ——————————————————————————————————————

5. Have you extended this approach to your class in general?

    ——

6. How have you extended this approach? *(please tick)*:
    [   ]   direct teaching of the method to the class.
    [   ]   making/drawing traffic light mottos for display.
    [   ]   assisting different children to use the method for solving particular soc problems.
    [   ]   using the method yourself to handle problems with your pupils.
    [   ]   other ways*(please specify)* ——————————————————————————

    ——

7. Will you continue/try the STOP-THINK-DO approach with:
    [   ]   the target child?
    [   ]   your class?

Bibliography

Allen, G.J., Chinsky, J.M., Larcen, S.W., Lochman, J.E., and Selinger, H.V., (1976). *Community Psychology and the Schools: A Behaviourally Oriented Multi-Level Preventive Approach.* Hillsdale, New Jersey: Earlbaum.

Asher, S.R. & Renshaw, P.D. (1981). Children without friends: Social knowledge and social skills training. In S.R. Asher & J.M. Gottman (Eds.), *The Development of Children's Friendships* (pp.273-296) New York: Cambridge University Press.

Bagarozzi, D. (1985). Implications of social skills training for social and interpersonal competence. In L.L 'Abate & M.A. Milan (Eds.). *Handbook of Social Skills Training and Research.* (pp.219-244). U.S.A: Wiley.

Barclay, J.R. (1966). Interest patterns associated with measures of social desirability. *Personnel and Guidance Journal,* 45,56-60.

Bellack, A.S., (1979). Behavioural assessment of social skills. In A.S. Bellack & M. Hersen (Eds.). *Research and Practice in Social Skills Training.* New York: Plenum Press.

Budd, K.S. (1985). Parents as mediators in the social skills training of children. In L.L. 'Abate & M.A. Milan (Eds.),*Handbook of Social Skills Training and Research.* (pp.245-262). U.S.A: Wiley.

Butler, L. & Meichenbaum, D. (1981). The assessment of interpersonal problemsolving skills. In P.C. Kendall & S.D. Hollon (Eds.),*Assessment Strategies for Cognitive-Behavioural Interventions.* (pp.197-225) New York: Academic Press.

Christoff, K.A., Scott, W.O.N., Kelly, M.L., Schlundt, D., Baer, G. & Kelly, J.A. (in press). Social skills and social problem solving training for extremely shy young adolescents. *Behaviour Therapy.*

Coie, J.D. & Kupersmidt, J.B. (1983). A behavioural analysis of emerging social status in boy's groups. *Child Development.* 54,1400-1416.

Combs, M.L. & Slaby, D.A. (1977). Social skills training with children. In B.B. Lahey & A.E. Kazdin (Eds.),*Advances in Clinical Child Psychology* 1,(pp.161-206). New York: Plenum Press.

Cowen, E.L., Pederson, A., Babigian, H., Izzo, L.D., & Trost, M.A. (1973). Long term follow-up of early detected vulnerable children. *Journal of Consulting and Clinical Psychology,* 41,438-446.

Cox, R.D., Gunn, W.B. & Cox, M.J. (1976). A film assessment and comparison of the social skilfulness of behaviour problem and non-problem male children. Paper presented at the meeting of the Association for Advancement of Behaviour Therapy, New York.

Dinkmeyer, D. & McKay, G.D. (1976). *Systematic Training for Effective Parenting.* Minnesota: AGS.

Dinkmeyer, D. & McKay, G.D. (1983). *Step/Teen Systematic Training for Effective Parenting of Teens.* Minnesota: AGS.

Dodge, K.A. (1983). Behavioural antecedents of peer social status: *Child Development*, 54, 1386-1399.

Dreikurs, R. & Soltz, V. (1972). *Happy Children. A Challenge to Parents*. Glasgow: Fontana.

Elias, M.J., Gara, M., Ubriaco, M., Rothbaum, P.A., Clabby, J.F. & Schuyler, T. (1986). Impact of a preventive social problem solving intervention on children's coping with middle-school stressors. *American Journal of Community Psychology*, 14,3,259-275.

Furnham, A. (1986). Social skills training with adolescents and young adults. In C.R. Hollin & P.Trower (Eds.). *Handbook of Social Skills Training*. 1,(pp.33-58) U.K: Pergamon Press.

Foster, S. (1983). Critical elements in the development of children's social skills. In R. Ellis & D. Whitington (Eds.). *New Directions in Social Skills Training* (pp.227-265). Kent: Croom Helm.

Freedman, B.J., Rosenthal, L., Donahue, C.P.Jr., Schlundt, D.G. & McFall, R.M. (1978). A social-behavioural analysis of skill deficits in delinquent and non-delinquent adolescent boys. *Journal of Consulting and Clinical Psychology*, 46,1448-1462.

French, D.C. & Tyne, T.F. (1982). The identification and treatment of children with peer-relationship difficulties. In J.P. Curran & P.M. Monti (Eds.). *Social Skills Training: A practical Handbook for Assessment and Treatment*. (pp.280-308) New York: Guilford Press.

Gesten, E.L., Rains, M.H., Rapkin, B.D., Weissberg, R.P., de Apodaca, R.F., Cowen, E.L. & Bowen, R. (1982). Training children in social problem-solving competencies: A first and second look. *American Journal of Community Psychology*, 10,1,95-115.

Gordon, T. (1970). *P.E.T. Parent Effectiveness Training*. New York: Plume.

Hartup, W.W. (1970). Peer interaction and social organization. In P. Mussen (Ed.). *Carmichael's Manual of Child Psychology* (Vol.2) New York: Wiley.

Herbert, M. (1986). Social skills training with children. In C.R. Hollin & P. Trower (Eds.). *Handbook of Social Skills Training*. 1,(pp.11-32), U.K: Pergamon Press.

Hops, H. (1983). Children's social competence and skill: Current research practices and future directions. *Behaviour Therapy*, 14,3-18.

Horowitz, L.M., French, R. & Anderson, C.A. (1982). The prototype of a lonely person. In L.A. Peplan & D. Perlman (Eds.). *Loneliness: A Source-book of Current Theory, Research and Therapy*. (pp.183-206) New York: Wiley-Interscience.

Hymel, S. & Asher, S.R. (1977). Assessment and training of isolated children's social skills. Paper presented at the biennial meeting of the society for Research in Child Development, New Orleans.

Hymel, S. & Rubin, K.H. (1985). Children with peer relationship and social skills problems: Conceptual, methodological, and developmental issues. In G.J. Whitehurst (Ed.),*Annals of Child Development*, 2,(pp.251-297). Greenwich, C.T. JAI Press.

Kazdin, A.E. (1985). *Treatment of Antisocial Behaviour in Children and Adolescents*. Illinois: Dorsey press.

Kazdin, A.E. (1987). Treatment of anti-social behaviour in children: Current status and future directions. *Psychological Bulletin*, 102,2,187-203.

Kazdin, A.E., Esveldt-Dawson, K., French, N.H., Unis, A.S. (1987). Problem-solving skills training and relationship therapy in the treatment of antisocial child behaviour. *Journal of Consulting and Clinical Psychology*, 55,1,76-85.

Kazdin, A.E., Esveldt-Dawson, K., French, N.H., Unis, A.S. (1987). Effects of parent management training and problem solving skills training combined in the treatment of antisocial child behaviour. *Journal of American Academy Child and Adolescent Psychiatry*, 26,3,416-424.

Kelly, J.A. & Hansen, D.J. (1987). Social interactions and adjustment. In V. Van Hasselt & M. Hersen (Eds.),*Handbook of Adolescent Psychology*. (pp.131-146) New York: Pergamon.

Kendall, P.C., Pellegrini, D.S. & Urbain, E.S. (1981). Approaches to assessment for cognitive behavioural interventions with children. In P.C. Kendall & S.D. Hollon (Eds.),*Assessment Strategies for Cognitive-Behavioural Interventions* (pp.227-285) New York: Academic Press.

Kendall, P.C. & Braswell, L. (1982). Cognitive-behavioural self-control therapy for children: A components analysis. *Journal of Consulting and Clinical Psychology*, 50,5,672-689.

Kendall, P.C., (1984). Annotation: Cognitive-behavioural self-control therapy for children. *Journal of Child Psychology & Psychiatry*, 25,2,173-179.

Kendall, P.C. & Braswell, L. (1985). Cognitive-Behavioural Therapy for Impulsive Children. New York: Guilford Press.

Kendall, P.C., (1985). Toward a cognitive-behavioural model of child psychopathology and a critique of related interventions. *Journal of Abnormal Child Psychology*, 13,3,357-372.

Krantz, M., Webb, S.D. & Andrews, D. (1984). The relationship between child and parental social competence. *Journal of Psychology*, 118,51-56.

Krasnor, L.R. & Rubin, K.H. (1981). The assessment of social problem-solving skills in young children. In T. Merluzzi, C. Glass & M. Genest (Eds.), *Cognitive Assessment*. (pp.452-476) New York: Guilford Press.

Ladd, G.W. (1981) Effectiveness of a social learning method for enhancing children's social interaction and peer acceptance. *Child Development*, 52,171-178.

Ladd, G.W. & Mize, J. (1983). A cognitive social learning model of social skill training. *Psychological Review*, 90,2,127-157.

Ladd, G.W. & Asher, S.R. (1985). Social skills training and children's peer relations. In L.L. 'Abate & M.A. Milan (Eds.),*Handbook of Social Skills Training and Research*. (pp.219-244). U.S.A: Wiley.

Lochman, J.E., Burch, P.R., Curry, J.F. & Lampron, L.B. (1984) Treatment and generalization effects of cognitive-behavioural and goal setting interventions with aggressive boys. *Journal of Consulting and Clinical Psychology*, 52,5,915-916.

Masten, A.S., Morison, P. & Pellegrini, D.S. (1985). A revised class play method of peer assessment. *Developmental Psychology*, 21,3,523-533.

McGillivray, J. (1983). Cognitive behaviour modification of impulsive responding by hyper-aggressive children in interpersonal problem situations. M. Psych. thesis, Latrobe University, Melbourne.

Meichenbaum, D., Henshaw, D., Himel, N. (1983). Coping with stress as a problem-solving process. In W. Krohne & L. Laux (Eds.),*Achievement, Stress and Anxiety*. Washington D.C: Hemisphere Press.

Muma, J.R. (1968). Peer evaluation and academic achievement in performance classes. *Personnel and Guidance Journal*, 46,580-585.

O'Connor, R.D. (1972). The relative efficacy of modelling, shaping, and the combined procedures for modification of social withdrawal. *Journal of Abnormal Psychology*, 79,327-334.

Oden, S.L. & Asher, S.R. (1977) Coaching children in social skills for friendship-making. *Child Development*, 48,495-506.

Parker, J.G. & Asher, S.R. (1987). Peer relations and later personal adjustment: Are low-accepted children at risk? *Psychological Bulletin*, 102,3,357-389.

Parkhurst, J.T. & Asher, S.R. (1985). Goals and concerns. Implications for the study of children's social competence. In B.B. Lahey & A.E. Kazdin (Eds.), *Advances in Clinical Child Psychology*, Vol.8. New York: Plenum Press.

Patterson, G.R., Chamberlain, P. & Reid, J.B. (1982). A comparative evaluation of a parent training programme. *Behaviour Therapy*, 13,638-650.

Pelham, W.E. & Bender, M.E. (1982). Peer relationships in hyperactive children: Description and treatment. In K.D. Gadgow & I.Bialer (Eds.), *Advances in Learning and Behavioural Disabilities*, 1,(pp.365-436). Greenwich CT:JAI Press.

Pellegrini, D.S. & Urbain, E.S. (1985). An evaluation of interpersonal cognitive problem solving with children. *Journal of Child Psychology and Psychiatry*, 26,1,17-41.

Pellegrini, D.S., Masten, A.S., Garmezy, N. & Ferrarese, M.J. (1987) Correlates of social and academic competence in middle childhood. *Journal of Child Psychology and Psychiatry*. 28,5,699-714.

Putallaz, M. (1983). Predicting children's sociometric status from their behaviour. *Child Development*, 54,1417-1426.

Renshaw, P.D. & Asher, S.R. (1983)Children's Goals and strategies for social interaction,*Merrill Palmer Quarterly*, 29,353-374.

Rickel, A.V., Eshelman, A.K. & Loigman, G.A. (1983). Social problem solving training: A Follow-up study of cognitive and behavioural effects. *Journal of Abnormal Child Psychology* 11,1,15-28.

Robins, L.N. (1966)*Deviant Children Grown Up*. Baltimore: Williams & Wilkins.

Roff, M., Sells, S.S. & Golden, M.M. (1972). *Social Adjustment and Personality Development in children*. Minneapolis: University of Minnesota Press.

Sabornie, E.J. & Ellis, E.S. (1987). Sociometry for teachers of behaviourally disordered students In R.B. Rutherford Jnr., C.M. Nelson & S.R. Forness (Eds.). *Severe Behaviour Disorders o Children and Youth*. (pp.28-40). Mass. U.S.A: Little Brown & Co.

Schrodt, G.R. Jnr. & Fitzgerald, B.A. (1987). Cognitive therapy with adolescents. *American Journal of Psychotherapy*, XL1,3,402-408.

Shure, M.B. & Spivack, G. (1978). *Problem Solving Techniques in Child Rearing*. San Francisco Jossey-Bass.

Singleton, L.C. & Asher, S.R. (1977). Peer preferences and social interaction among third-grade children in an integrated school district. *Journal of Educational Psychology*, 69,330-336.

Siperstein, G.M. & Gale, M.E. (1983). Improving peer relationships of rejected children. Pape presented at the biennial meeting of the Society for Research in Child Development, Detroit, MI

Spivack, G. & Shure, M.B. (1974). *Social Adjustment of Young Children: A Cognitive Approac to Solving Real-life Problems*. San Francisco: Jossey-Bass.

Stark, K.D., Reynolds, W.M. & Kaslow, N.J. (1987). A comparison of the relative efficacy o self-control therapy and behavioural problem-solving therapy for depression in children. *Journa of Abnormal Child Psychology*, 15,1,91-113.

Strain, P.S. & Fox, J.J. (1981). Peer social initiations and the modification of social withdrawal: A Review and future perspective. *Journal of Pediatric Psychology*, 6,4,417-433.

Taylor, A.R. & Asher, S.R. (1984). Children's goals and social competence: Individual difference in a game-playing context. In T. Field, J.L. Roopnarine & M. Segal (Eds.). *Friendship in Norma and Handicapped Children* (pp.53-77). Norwood, New Jersey: Ablex.

Van Hasselt, V.B., Hersen, M., Whitehill, M.B. & Bellack, A.S. (1979)Social skills assessment an training for children: An evaluative review. *Behaviour Research and Therapy*, 17,413-437.

Weissberg, R.P., Gesten, E.L., Carnrike, C.L., Toro, P.A., Rapkin, B.D. Davidson, E. & Cower E.L. (1981). Social problem-solving skills training: A competence-building intervention wit second- to fourth-grade children. *American Journal of Community Psychology*, 9,4,411-423.

Wheeler, V.A. & Ladd, G.W. (1982)Assessment of children's self-efficacy for social interactions with peers. *Developmental Psychology*, 18,795-805.

ADDITIONAL RESOURCE MATERIALS.

"What Should I Do?" Film Series, (1985) Walt Disney Educational Media Co. Available from Focal Communications Pty. Ltd, 123 Clarence St., Sydney, New South Wales.

Camp, B.W. & Bash, M.A. (1981) *Think Aloud: Increasing Social and Cognitive Skills. - A Problem Solving Programme for Children.* Primary Level. Illinois, Research Press.

Dinkmeyer, D. & McKay, G. (1976). *Systematic Training for Effective Parenting.* Minnesota, AGS.

Dinkmeyer, D. & McKay, G.D. (1983). *STEP/Teen Systematic Training for Effective Parenting of Teens.* Minnesota, AGS.

Dinkmeyer, D., McKay, G., Dinkmeyer, D. Jr., Dinkmeyer, J. & McKay, J.L. (1987). *The Next Step Effective Parenting through Problem Solving.* Minnesota, AGS.

Dupont, H. Gardner, O. & Brady, D. (1974). *Toward Affective Development.* Minnesota, AGS.

Gordon, T. (1970)*P.E.T. Parent Effectiveness Training.* New York: Plume.